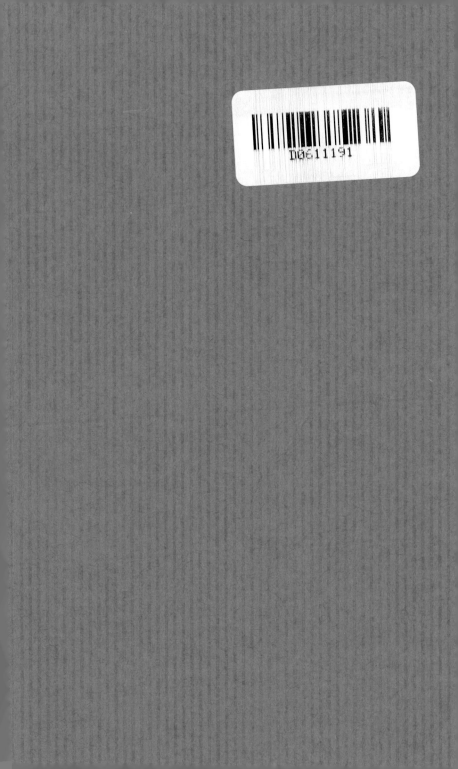

And God Created Wrinkles

Also by E. Jane Mall

Kitty, My Rib
Beyond the Rummage Sale
Abingdon Manual of Installation Services
A Mother's Gifts
How to Become Wealthy Publishing a Newsletter

And God Created Wrinkles

E. JANE MALL

Foreword by Eugenia Price

A Ballantine/Epiphany Book
Ballantine Books • New York

A Ballantine/Epiphany Book

Library of Congress Cataloging-in-Publication Data

Mall, E. Jane, 1920–
    And God created wrinkles.

    "A Ballantine/Epiphany book."
    Bibliography: p.
    1. Aged women—United States—Life skills guides.
2. Aged women—United States—Psychology. 3. Aged
women—United States—Attitudes. I. Title.
HQ1064.U5M33   1988   305.4   87-47854
ISBN 0-345-34746-3

Design by Holly Johnson
Manufactured in the United States of America

First Edition: May 1988
10 9 8 7 6 5 4

Dedicated to

Ellen Flaskamper, who has been my friend, mentor, sister in Christ, and who is a beautiful old lady.

Author's note: This book is my love letter to old ladies. If any of you young whippersnappers give this book to an old lady as a gift, please do it in the same spirit; along with the book, give a hug and a kiss!

ejm

A very special, loving thanks to Toni Simmons, who is a writer's dream editor.

Contents

Foreword by Eugenia Price   xi

Preface   xiii

Section I: There Is Good News for Old Ladies   1

    Chapter 1: The Ripened Generation   3

    Chapter 2: Like Yourself and Live Longer   12

    Chapter 3: The Stages of Aging   17

    Chapter 4: Make the Most of the Rest of Your
       Life   26

    Chapter 5: A Look at Ecclesiastes   30

Section II: Getting Personal: Be Good to Your-
    self; You're Worth It   39

    Chapter 6: You Are Not a Nobody   41

    Chapter 7: Try New Challenges   49

    Chapter 8: Be Honest with Yourself   59

    Chapter 9: Live Your Life as It Pleases You   65

    Chapter 10: Develop the Habit of Hope   71

    Chapter 11: Work Toward a Better You   76

    Chapter 12: Grow in Your Faith   88

Chapter 13: How to Make the Most of Each
    Day   91
Section III: How to Get Along with Family and
    Friends   97
Chapter 14: Treasure Your Independence   99
Chapter 15: Keep Friends in Your Life   106
Chapter 16: Stop Playing Games with Your
    Children   118
Chapter 17: Don't Be an Old Lady Manip-
    ulator   123
Chapter 18: Living with Your Children   133
Chapter 19: Grandparenting   139
Chapter 20: Practice the Art of Listening   148
Section IV: How to Maintain a Right Attitude   153
Chapter 21: Believe in Yourself   155
Chapter 22: Just Because It's Old Doesn't
    Mean It's Good   160
Chapter 23: Love, Sex, Dating, Remarriage   165
Chapter 24: Never Lose Hope   176
Chapter 25: Build Your Confidence and De-
    stroy Your Fears   179
Section V: How You Can Prepare for Death   185
Chapter 26: Living in the Past   187
Chapter 27: The Need to Prepare for Death   191
Chapter 28: Write Your Will   199
Chapter 29: Some Thoughts About Dust   204
Chapter 30: One Person's Choice   209
Chapter 31: Is Suicide an Answer?   214

Section VI: Discover New Things to Do   223
   Chapter 32: Write a Family History   225
   Chapter 33: A Checklist on Your Progress 228
   Chapter 34: Potpourri   232
   Chapter 35: Why Don't You . . .   244
Afterglow   247
Recommended Reading   249

Foreword

At some point this year I plan to sign a publisher's contract for two more long historical novels, each of which will use up at least two years of my remaining time on earth. When you read this I will be seventy-two. Jane Mall was a mere sixty-five when she wrote this superb volume, and yet she has said it all and I am cheering! Of course we're getting old and of course sometimes it's boring and sometimes it hurts, but it's natural—it's part of God's scheme of things and I wouldn't change places with a younger me for anything in this world or the next. There's a good kind of peace and a vast new store of energy in just realizing that in our sixties, seventies, or eighties we have indeed learned something from most of those early mistakes. I like being an "old lady" and I find, now that I've smiled and applauded my way through Jane's superior book, I like being an "old lady" even more. Her past life and mine have not been even similar in their circumstances, but on the subject of aging in God's presence and the presence of all those smart enough to seek out our company, Jane Mall and I agree totally. Whatever your age, read *And God Created Wrinkles*. If not now, someday; as sure as the sun keeps rising, you'll be sorry if you miss it.

Eugenia Price
author of the bestselling
Savannah Quartet

Preface

I am not an expert on the subject of old age, and I don't pretend to be. I do know what it's like to grow old.

Unless you have been there, you don't know what it's like.

Nothing in this book advises you to ignore your age or pretend that you're not growing old. On the contrary, my advice is to face it, admit it, and learn how to cope with it.

That's one of the reasons I am getting fed up with all the silly titles people are dreaming up for us. I refuse to play that game. I was a baby, a teenager, a young woman, a middle-aged woman, and now I am an old woman. You don't have to make up a title for me in order for me to feel better about myself.

I would like to see more and more old women admit that they're old ladies and show pride in the fact. I want to see them dressed to the nines, with makeup, the latest hairstyle, telling the world: "Sure,

I'm an old lady, but look at what I have accomplished! Look at what I'm doing!" We can give the title OLD LADY a new meaning.

My daughter Heide is a checker in a supermarket. One day an old lady came through her line and dropped her change. "Oh dear," she said, "I am such an old lady!"

Heide said, "My mom says you should be proud to be an old lady. She is. She says she's proud because she knows what it took to get to where she is."

The old lady said, "Well, I never thought about it like that, but I guess that's the truth."

In this book, I have tried to put forth a new concept of old age.

When my dear friend Flash goes grocery shopping, I love to watch her. Up and down the aisles this little old lady goes, and in her wake she leaves many smiles. She talks to this person and that one, throwing comments over her shoulder as if she were tossing confetti around. She is completely unaware of the marvelous impression she makes. She is just having a good time, but she makes me proud to be an old lady.

My daughter in Oregon called the other night and asked me two questions. The first one was "Mom, why did you write *And God Created Wrinkles?*"

My first response was, "Marie, it's my love letter to old ladies."

Well, it is, but it's a lot more than that. I love old ladies, and the more of them I meet, the more I love them. So many have such great stories to tell, such uplifting, inspirational things to relate. Besides, I'm an old lady, too, and my interest is far from superficial.

However, as the writing of this book progressed, and as I talked to more and more old ladies, things changed. The book became more than just a love letter.

The reason for this was that I was talking to more old ladies, making a point of doing this, sometimes going out of my way for an exchange of words.

A rather amazing thing happened. I realized that the old ladies had sort of divided themselves into two distinct groups.

In group one were the cheerful, upbeat women who generated happiness and goodwill and seemed eager to learn and experience new things. These were the ones I wanted to take home with me. I could write a love letter to them.

Then there were the complainers, and it was evident with their first words. In response to "How are you?" or "May I help you?" they recited a litany of ailments. Some told me exactly what their blood pressure reading was (the highest their doctor had ever seen). Others went into detail about their latest illness ("I will never be the same again") or operation ("The doctors were amazed that I lived through it").

If I hung around long enough (I usually didn't), these ladies swung into details about how their children treated them (rotten), how their appetite was (terrible), and how nobody cared a fig about them.

At first I tried countering their negative words with positive ones. "My kids are very good to me." ("You're one of the lucky ones. Oh, count your blessings, dear.")

"I don't have a car either, so I take a taxi when I want to go someplace." ("Oh, aren't you lucky! I can't afford taxis!")

I ask myself, Why? What made the difference? It had little to do with anything physical: I met some old ladies in wheelchairs and on crutches who were as cheerful as a sunny day.

It had nothing to do with money. Some of the biggest gripers and complainers had diamonds sparkling on nearly every finger.

I talked to these ladies in supermarkets, in shopping malls, at the beach, and in church. No matter where I met them, the ratio was about the same. I am sorry to relate that the complainers outnumbered the glad ones.

What made the difference? And what could I write that would help?

Marie had asked me why I wrote *And God Created Wrinkles.* I looked at myself. I am a happy, active old lady. I do not feel sorry for myself (hardly ever), and I have come to the conclusion that prolonged loneliness is a form of self-indulgence. And believe me, if I told you the story of my life (I won't), you would not believe the horror of many parts of it. In some ways, I have had a hard life. I have also lived through much that is good. Still, I am a content old lady.

I am not one of the brightest people in the world, but I'm not stupid, either. I have a strong faith, but it wavers often. With each passing year, I realize how far from perfection I am.

So wherein lies the answer? I believe the most important thing we can do is to develop a positive attitude about everything. Live with hope and a positive attitude and you will be a content old lady. My sister-in-law had surgery recently. She said, "Now I must concentrate on a positive, healing attitude." We should do this all the time. I have tried to put forth this philosophy in nearly every chapter in this book.

Marie's second question was: "I'm thirty-three years old. I'm beginning to get varicose veins. There isn't much I can do about growing old, is there? It's just going to happen no matter what I do."

I thought about that a lot. No, there is nothing you can do about wrinkles and sagging flesh, but young women certainly can start preparing for a gratifying old age. And they can start now, no matter what their age, because it is the inner woman who will triumph over the flesh in the long run. If you are a mean-tempered, stingy, selfish, complaining young woman, I hate to think what you will be like when you're old.

Nourish your good attributes: your even temper, your generosity, your love for so many things and people, your humor. Let them grow as you grow, and you will be a beautiful old lady.

Now I realize that this book is more than a love letter to old ladies. I don't know all the answers, but I have wrestled with the problems of growing old and I have come up with some solutions.

So come along with me, dear old ladies. We will begin with the knowledge that God did indeed create wrinkles, and all the other parts of us, and discover, with me, that the last of life can be a wonderful, happy experience.

There Is Good News for Old Ladies

CHAPTER I:

The Ripened Generation

Some have said that calling us the Ripened Generation brings to mind overripe fruit, rotting, ready to fall from the tree. I don't see it that way at all. I think of ripened fruit as being at the very peak of perfection. The fruit has survived the onslaughts of weather and the attacks of insects. It has ripened, reached the height of flavor, fulfilled its purpose and promise. It has never been as good as it is right now or ever will be again. Of course, it is approaching the end, but at the moment it hangs on the tree in all its glory.

We are the Ripened Generation. We, too, have weathered the storms and withstood the onslaughts of life, and we have survived. We are nearing the end, but we are ripe and we have never been as good as we are right now.

The popular saying "Old age is not for sissies" is true. Growing old is a devastating experience. It's cruel in some ways, and demeaning and humbling. But

3

. . . is that all there is to growing old? Are there any positive aspects?

If we are lucky enough to reach old age, we have to learn how to cope with it. There is no magic cure or miracle pill that can restore our youth, so we have to make the best of what we are. We can try to make these last years our best years.

There is no pattern to the stages of growing old. Many things, emotional and physical, intervene to render the experience different for each of us. It was not always like that. Until recently, the state of old age didn't last long enough to present many problems. When my grandmother was younger than I am now, only in her fifties, she was an old woman. She wore long skirts and button shoes and she was more or less relegated to her rocking chair in the corner. That corner was in the home of her married son.

Today we are not considered old at such an early age, and we are not sitting quietly in a corner of someone else's home. Many of us are still active at jobs and community projects. Most of us live independently alone and drive our cars and have a pretty good time. Retiring to a rocker is a long way down the road for us.

Still, we expend a great deal of energy in learning how to cope with the loneliness of old age. In this book, we will probe some creative ways of handling loneliness as well as some other negative aspects of growing old. If we are reasonably healthy, and most of us are, there is no reason why our last years can't be happy years.

The most awesome fact most of us face is that we are losing so much that is dear, familiar, and comforting. We lose husbands and jobs; our eyesight and hearing fail us. We lose our teeth and our figures and our independence. Our friends die and our children move away. After a lifetime of acquiring new things and new experiences, and of keeping what we have, it's a great shock to be losing so much. How we cope with these inevitable losses largely determines the quality of our ripening years.

Nobody has to tell us that we are in the final stage of life. We know that and we want to deal with this reality in the best possible way. We have no idea what may happen to change our lives, and we worry a little about that. It makes us cautious. The only certainty in our lives now is our death, and we think about it, prepare for it, but we don't dwell on it. Later we'll look at some options for those preparations.

What we must dwell on is living as full and as productive a life as possible. We can do it. I talk to old ladies all the time. I seek them out wherever I go, and they continue to amaze me with their uplifting spirit and their eagerness to learn.

That's what *And God Created Wrinkles* is about. Some years ago I eliminated sugar and salt from my diet—one-half teaspoon at a time. It was a painless discipline. I believe that you, no matter what your age, can improve your ripening years in the same way. We can take our life one day at a time. We can eliminate some of the old ways, the nonproductive thoughts and habits, and just as gradually introduce new, spiritually healthful things. It's certainly worth a try—and it is my hope and my prayer that this book will give you some ideas on how to do it.

None of us likes to be tagged or labeled. I get turned off when I hear people talk about senior citizens. Don't ask me to join your group if it's called Spares 'n Pairs, because you have tagged me a spare. I already feel like a fifth wheel too often. However, since this book is directed to older women, I should explain something. Throughout, I use the term "old lady." I mean it in the finest sense. I think of myself as an old lady. I am old and I am a lady—believe it!

Sometimes I refer to myself as "an old lady," and I immediately get the response: "Oh, you're not an old lady. Don't call yourself that. You're as young as you feel."

I simply can't buy that. I don't see anything wrong in being called an old lady, since that is what I am. I believe that one of the first things we have to do is to face facts and stop pretending we're something we're not.

Some have suggested we be called the Mature Generation. That's fairly accurate, but the term I like best is the Ripened Generation. We are ripe as opposed to green and unfinished. (Yes, ripened fruit is close to the end of life, but while it's ripe, it's at its best. We old ladies are at our peak of perfection.) We have never been this good.

I live in a beautiful South Texas town on the Gulf of Mexico, and I see a peculiar sight nearly every day that makes me laugh. Little groups of sea gulls are always fighting over some dirty puddle in a parking lot. Only a minute's flight away is a vast, sparkling body of water! Too often, we are like that. We moan, "Oh, if only I were young again!" "If only . . . If only . . ." when inside each of us there are vast resources for enjoying this part of our lives to the fullest. I hope this book will help some old ladies understand how to tap these resources.

We are an expanding, growing minority today. Approximately twenty-eight million Americans are over sixty-five, and there are over ten million widows in the United States. Our number is growing—yet nobody is paying much attention to us except to worry about what they're going to do with us as we grow older and older. Sometimes we get the feeling that we are being extremely inconsiderate in hanging around for so long. We aren't too worried about it, though. We can take care of ourselves fairly well; we want to remain independent; we hope that our money lasts as long as we do.

In shopping malls, restaurants, and airports, gray heads and thickening waistlines are a common sight. Despite our number, all I see on TV, in the newspapers, and in the magazines are young faces, young hair, young bodies. Once in a while I come across an old face, but it is usually in an ad for laxatives or something to ease the pain of hemorrhoids or arthritis.

It seems that once you pass a certain age, you don't count for much. According to most of the ads, all we eat is bran and prunes. All the women jumping up and down doing aerobics at the spas are young and thin. They invite me, "no matter what your age," to join them. Surely they jest. Show me someone with thinning gray hair and no waistline and a sagging, overweight body in that spa, and I might consider joining.

Most of the latest fashions would make us look idiotic. We are here, in vast numbers, but nobody is paying much attention to us. Maybe we should be called the Ignored Generation.

I wonder how the next batch of older women, the ones who are young now, will handle old age. In a way, I wish I could be around to watch, because they are different from us. Members of our generation were raised in families where the father ruled the roost. When I married, I knew from the start that my husband was the boss.

Oh, I stood up for "my rights" more than my mother did, but not much. The thing is, this new batch of women has experienced women's lib, making them a lot different from us. It will be interesting to see how they handle old age, especially since they will probably live even longer than we do now.

Some older women say that we are not very different from those lovelies in the magazines and on TV. "We have just lived longer, that's all."

Oh, come on! Give me a break! We are different in so many ways. Most of us are smarter. After all, we have already committed our youthful, foolish mistakes and have witnessed the results. We don't have the energy that young women have, nor the same interests. We don't think like the young women of today. Instead of trying to fool ourselves into thinking we are just like them, I suggest that we celebrate the differences.

Some young people are put off by the elderly. I believe we can change that. When I was young, I didn't like being around old people. I didn't want to touch them or be touched by them. Old age, with its wrinkles and sagging flesh, was not at all attractive to me. I couldn't explain it then and can't now, but the attitude was very real.

Now that I am old, I see this same shrinking away from me in the eyes of some young people, and it hurts. I wonder if that's how lepers felt. I feel as though my gray hair and wrinkled skin represent a communicable disease. Perhaps this feeling in young people is born of an inherent fear. They know that they, too, will grow old, and they don't want to look at or get too near its presence. Maybe we can help them see that being old is not a disease. That it can be, in fact, a lot of fun. The best years, in a way.

For a while I pitied myself a lot. I pouted and shed some silent tears. And then, at just about the time my skin lost its elasticity, my hair lost its color, and my big, brown eyes receded into my eyelids, my children decided that they didn't need me anymore.

I am still an excellent typist, and my memory is as sharp as that of a young person, but I certainly wouldn't have the nerve to apply for a job.

Poor me! I was growing old and refusing to grow up. Then I read in the Bible something that gave me a new direction.

> The aged women likewise, that they be in behavior as becometh holiness, not false accusers, not given to much wine, teachers of good things; that they may teach the young women to be sober, to love their husbands, to love their children. (Titus 2:3–4)

That's a tall order. "Behavior as becometh holiness" makes me feel that I could be important after all. If I'm not too old to try, that is.

Still, it gives me some direction. Maybe I am not so outmoded and ready for the trash pile as I imagined.

If we can show young women of today, by our example, what happens if you live a sober life, if you love others, and if you keep your wits about you, we will be teachers of good things.

When my daughter gets on her high horse and is impatient and angry with me and I respond with love, I am demonstrating forgiving love.

When my son just plain ignores my existence for long periods of time and I don't reprimand him, but greet him with welcoming arms, I am showing him what patient love is. I can be a teacher of good things.

Being an old lady comes as a sort of surprise. It first dawned on me when I read about a woman in the newspaper. The reporter referred to her as an "elderly woman." She was my age, and I did a double take. That's me! I am an elderly woman. Many things happen in our later years that come as a surprise. We are simply not prepared for our old age. That is my reason for writing this book. It helps to look at what happens, to share our experiences, and to see what others have done. Some old ladies are victorious and some are miserable failures. We can look at both of them and decide how we can be the former and avoid being the latter.

CHAPTER 2:

Like Yourself and Live Longer

You can stare at snapshots of yourself when you were young and thin and pretty and feel sorry for yourself because now you're old and wrinkled. Or you can be like my friend Flash, who says, "Jane, we are a couple of beautiful old broads."

It's important to have a good opinion of yourself, to consider this stage of your life as a new adventure, one you will make the most of. Be realistic; accept the fact that you are old and getting older. Resolve to live life to the fullest.

If you are thinking that old age is a plateau you have reached, think again. Plateaus are periods of no progress. You have reached many plateaus in your life-time. You received the promotion for which you worked so hard; there was finally enough money in your savings account for a down payment on a house; you completed a course of study; you gave birth to your last child. Plateaus. Reaching a goal. Then on to the next goal.

Old age is a plateau, of course, but if you view it as the end of life, the end of your responsibility, if you see no more challenges, you're headed nowhere. Plateaus are brief resting places. Age has changed your goals, that's all. It hasn't eliminated the necessity for them. Don't sit in a corner and feel sorry for yourself. Move into this next phase of life and keep an open, expectant mind. New adventures and challenges await you.

The truth is, old age is looking better and better and lasting longer and longer. Since this is a new phenomenon, people are watching us, wondering what we are going to do and what they will have to do with us.

They are discovering a few surprises. Some of the myths of old age are being shot down.

We can't be put into a set pattern or mold. Some of us are physically active, while some sit and watch TV. Some can paint and write and act in amateur theater. Some generally stay home. We're not homogeneous, and this fact puzzles the experts.

Another thing that is coming to light as we live longer and longer is the fact that nearly all of our mental faculties remain intact, as good as ever, as long as our health does. We have to continually exercise our minds by reading, working crossword puzzles, learning new things. Jog or walk every day, climb steps, stretch once or twice a day. The saying "Use it or lose it" applies to us.

There are even a few things we old people do better than young people. We have the advantage of experience in many different fields of interest, and that counts for a lot. In other words, we have paid our dues.

True, we are slower. Perhaps that comes from caution. Once I was running down an inclining walk covered with wet, newly cut grass and I slipped and fell. I tore some ligaments in my arm, which gave me aches and pain for a couple of years. I walk more slowly now, watching for what is underfoot. I don't walk slowly because I am old, but because I have learned from experience that it is a wise thing to do.

If our reflexes when driving are not as swift as those of the young, we should stay off the expressways. We move more slowly, but we don't rush headlong into situations, either. We have plenty of time, and we finally realize that we don't have to bother with so many things. Which means we don't have to waste time.

People laugh at old people who can't remember names or lists. All the young people I know have this same problem, but when they forget, it's funny or cute. When we do the same thing, it's old age creeping in.

Young people know every word of many of the lyrics of the latest rock hits, and we say, "Isn't that amazing?" I don't want to listen to those lyrics, much less memorize them, but I can recite poetry from my childhood, and I can still recite most of "Die Lorelie" in German.

I for one don't want to be compared to the young in everything I do, because it doesn't make much sense. I do some things better than they do, and if they would stop exalting speed, the experts might be in for a surprise. Perhaps I can't perform a certain task as fast as a young person can, but if I do it as well, what's the difference?

Young people act and react swiftly, it's true, but as they mature, or in order to mature, they have to lose some of that speed. It is necessary for them to slow down, to take a second look now and then. Those who grow up have to learn how to stop hurrying.

We learned this skill some time ago. We know it isn't necessary, or even advisable usually, to rush in and finish everything in a hurry. We know that often we save time by taking more time.

We are more patient than we have ever been, willing and able to consider all aspects of a situation or problem. In my book, that's better than being fast. There is a certain picture of old age that has been around for quite a while, but it seems to me that it is about time the picture be changed. The old stereotype simply isn't accurate. The experts who are studying us should look at us, and what we can do, and what we are doing, and stop comparing us with youth.

Bearing all of these things in mind, it is my hope

that you will accept this book as truly my love letter to you. When I see an old lady's eyes fill with tears as she says, "I'm so lonely I want to die!" . . .

Or see a lovely old lady cry, "I don't have anything to do!" . . .

Or watch old ladies cling to their children and lay blankets of guilt on them . . .

Or hear the cries of old ladies that always begin with "If only . . ." (I were young again/he were still alive . . . etc.) . . .

Or listen to old ladies use the excuse "I can't do that anymore" . . .

Then I want to go to each one and tell them they are wrong. I want to tell them how beautiful they are, how much there is still left to do.

No, we're not young anymore. Let's just accept that fact and get on with living.

CHAPTER 3:

The Stages of Aging

I read about a ninety-five-year-old woman who is a champion bowler and a woman nearing one hundred who climbs mountains; an eighty-three-year-old woman writes poetry that makes me laugh and cry in the same breath; another paints beautiful pictures of the sea. It's obvious that age doesn't necessarily inhibit accomplishment. Other stages of life have certain limitations; you can't practice law until you have passed the bar; you can't be a schoolteacher until you have completed the required education. You can't marry until you reach a certain age. You have to wait for a lot of things. You must grow up to them.

We're not bothered by these limitations. We are already grown up, and there is very little we can't do if we want to. Think of that. In a way, it's mind-blowing. Yes, there are stages of aging, but for the first time in our lives, we determine what stage we're in.

Of course, every part of life has its predictable stages. At a certain time, give or take a few months, a baby will crawl, walk, and talk. The teenage boy's voice will change, and a girl will menstruate. We recognize these stages of life, anticipate them, and know fairly well how to deal with them.

Growing old doesn't have any predictable stages. We all age differently, depending on a variety of factors. Some people are old at fifty, others are young at seventy. And there is a lot of variation in between.

Some things you can't help. If you are crippled with arthritis or have severe health problems, you are limited, just as any twenty-year-old would be limited with physical problems.

It would be wonderful if I could tell you that your attitude will make all the difference in how old you look and feel. Attitude makes a huge difference, of course, but it can't change everything.

Several things that happen to most of us give a hint that we're getting old:

• When you feel dizzy leaning over the sink to brush your teeth or wash your hair.
• When you have to get out of bed in the morning by easy stages: sit up and wait, put your feet on the floor and wait, finally stand up and wait. If everything seems to be working, you're on your feet and ready to move.
• Some old people sit and stare at a blank wall for fifteen or twenty minutes before they can get going.

That's all right. Stare. Wipe your mind free of sleep and dreams and gently lead it into another day.

I plug in the coffeepot, get out my juice and bottles of vitamins and calcium supplement, and then go out for the morning paper. If the paper is where it's supposed to be, my day is off to a good start. If it isn't there, I am almost reduced to tears. I know it's partly because I don't like having my routine interrupted, but it is also partly because for so many years I didn't have time to enjoy the morning paper with breakfast. There was seldom time for breakfast. I thank God every morning for the pleasure of being able to leisurely read my morning paper. By the way, it's helpful to get into the habit of noticing the pleasures and thanking God for them. You will discover many good things in each day.

You mellow out as the day progresses and perhaps take a walk, visit a friend, write a letter. You try to keep busy. It's a wonder you're tired enough to go to bed at night, but you are.

This routine can go on for a long enough time that we become comfortable with it; and there is nothing wrong with that. We're entitled to it. However, it's a good idea to vary your routine now and then, to shake it up a bit, so that when the inevitable changes occur, they won't throw you for a loop.

It's true that there are no predictable stages of growing old, but there are changes. For a long time we can perform certain physical feats very easily, and then the day comes when we can't. We took stairs two at a time if we were in a hurry; we climbed up a ladder and changed a light bulb and scrambled down again; when we rose from a sitting position we did it in one fluid motion, off and running as we rose; we sat cross-legged on the floor for hours. New limitations painfully remind us that we can't do these things any longer.

Remember eating fried foods whenever you felt like it? If food was greasy or spicy, or you ate too much, or feasted on gooey sundaes or boxes of chocolates, it didn't matter very much. Now it does. We have to say no to certain foods. Changes. It's no big deal. We learn to cope as these things happen to us.

Attitude makes a big difference in coping with these changes, as does retaining your sense of humor. Don't regard the changes as tragedies, because they aren't. In some ways you're better off now than when you were young.

Several manufacturers of pain relievers conducted a study and discovered that many pains decrease as a person ages. The older you get, the fewer colds you get; headaches and backaches and stomachaches decrease in frequency and intensity. Certainly premenstrual and menstrual pains are a thing of the past. We have less dental pain, because most of us have no teeth. And we are rid, finally, of the negative effects of stress. We don't have to worry about a job or the boss or our bank account and whether or not we have enough to pay the mortgage and car payments. So most of us are in pretty good shape and without a valid reason for not enjoying our old age.

Still, certain things do happen and our bodies change, but we handle it because we have to. We don't have a choice.

When I discovered that I had shrunk an inch in height, I told my children it was a big relief. "Now I know I won't die," I told them. "I'll just keep shrinking until there is nothing left."

One morning I went out early to check on my little strawberry patch. A bird swooped down in front of me, grabbed a large strawberry, and flew off with it. I yelled at that bird and my teeth flew out of my mouth. I plucked them out of the strawberry patch, dusted them off, and popped them back into my mouth. I was laughing at myself the rest of the day.

The next day I bought the stuff I needed to keep my teeth where they belonged.

One day I had a cold and my nose was dripping and my eyes watered and I sneezed nonstop. One particularly violent sneeze caught me by surprise, and I wet my pants. I told my daughter I was leaking at both ends. Certain muscles in our bodies lose their elasticity as we grow older. It's nothing to get excited about; it happens to all of us. I could have cried all day about that, but instead I bought a supply of panty liners and forgot about that little problem.

21

Whenever I take a bath or shower, I become a flaky old lady. My arms and legs flake as though I had a disease. So I buy body lotions, and rubbing them in has become a part of my bath routine. I don't want my skin flaking off. I need it to hold me together.

My hair gets dry and frizzy, so I rub some Wesson oil in it before I shampoo, and my hair is soft and shiny.

I know that my memory is not as sharp as it once was. One time I forgot which buttons to push to make the microwave oven work. My mind was a complete blank, and I had to call my daughter and ask her how to do it. It was a terrible, frightening experience because I had been using that microwave almost on a daily basis for three years. However, I learned the combination again, and I haven't forgotten it since. If I do, I have it written down so I won't have to let anyone know that I forgot again.

I forget names and sometimes have to wait a few hours or days before I can recall them.

In the middle of a sentence sometimes I forget what I was going to say.

Just about anything I don't write down is guaranteed to be forgotten. I keep a small notebook and pen with me at all times.

Forgetting has its advantages: I love to read mysteries, and I devour them. However, I will never run out of mysteries to read because a year after I have read one, I have forgotten who the killer was. So I read it again and enjoy it as much as I did the first time.

I can watch movies on TV over again because I don't remember seeing them the first time.

Old people are always portrayed moaning and groaning about their aching bones and joints. It's not a true picture. Most of the young people I know complain more than any old person I know. My son always greets me with a resumé of his health and his latest visit to the chiropractor. My daughter never fails to inform me of the status of the corns on her feet, her stomachaches, and how fat she is.

I have concluded that many of the stereotypes of old people are wrong, and certainly we don't want to contribute to that false picture. Accept the changes as and when they come, cope with them, and then move on to the next stage or change or whatever you want to call it. Do it with humor and patience, and thank God for them.

We are the ones who decide what kind of an old lady we will be. We can and should live our lives with dignity and independence.

We have lived long enough to know how critical patience is. It's important to know how to wait, and we know better than most. In our youth we wanted everything, and we wanted it yesterday. Our hearts beat fast with anticipation, and when we didn't get what we hoped for, our despondency was washed by tears. Over and over until we learned to wait, and then the highs weren't as high, but the lows didn't drag us down, either.

Our lives can be serene. We can refuse to do those things that don't please us and indulge ourselves in things that do.

I have no guilt pangs now when I refuse a request for my services and/or money. "I have done that for many years," I say, "and now I don't do that anymore." I don't get any arguments, either. It is apparent that I value myself and my life-style. We have earned the right to say no.

When I was young, I had many plans and hopes and dreams for the future. Oh, the things I was going to accomplish! Now the future is here and on its last legs, and I keep asking myself: What have I accomplished? Did I make any lasting mark? Did I do anything worthwhile?

My husband and many of my friends are dead. My children no longer need me, and when they do stop, now and then, to notice me, it's usually to mother me. "Let me carry that for you, Mom" and "Be careful of that step." Or "Did you forget your keys again?" I resent this treatment in a mild way. It seems condescending and patronizing.

When they were young, I took them everywhere I went: to the bowling alley, on picnics, to the movies. I wanted to do more for them than feed them and provide the necessary shelter and clothing. I wanted them to have fun, to know the joy of simple pleasures.

Now they don't include me in their fun activities because I am too old and too slow and I wouldn't fit in. That's right. I wouldn't fit in and I don't want to.

I saw a lady today with gray hair pulled back in a ponytail, wrinkled face heavy with makeup, flabby thighs squeezed into a pair of shorts. She was laughing with a group of young people, trying to keep up with them. I could have cried.

I have no desire to keep up with the younger generation. Although I do not have an abundance of material wealth, I have received other assets which I treasure. I have patience and tranquility, true independence, some wisdom that comes with maturity, a sense of dignity and finally, I know pretty much who I am and where I'm going (not far). These are some of the compensations we receive when our youth is gone. I am happy to step out of the way and leave the arena to the young. I know what I have accomplished and even though it's not exactly what I once dreamed about, I'm satisfied. I still have time to accomplish more.

What all of us should desire now is to show young people that old age is not frightening or sad, ugly or nonproductive. It doesn't even have to be dull.

As a joke, I recently suggested to my ninety-three-year-old mother-in-law that she take up bowling. She didn't smile. "Oh, I'm too busy to start anything like that," she responded. Now, that's the kind of old lady I want to be. Don't you?

CHAPTER 4:

Make the Most of the Rest of Your Life

I am a Christian feminist. I can't believe that any woman of today, regardless of her age, is not to some degree a feminist.

I do not believe that God made man, realized Her mistake, and then did it right and made woman.

However, I do believe that men and women are equal in the eyes of God. I do not believe that women are to be subservient to men. Genesis 1:27 says, "God created man in his own image . . . male and female."

Paul wrote of the very core of Christianity: "There is neither Jew nor Greek, there is neither male nor female, for ye are all one in Christ Jesus." (Galatians 3:28)

Jew or Gentile, male or female, we are created equal. Women's lib or no women's lib, I can live with that!

Despite some feminist gains, women—particularly widows—still don't feel entirely whole. We tend to feel that without a man, we are somehow not quite as important as we were with one.

Those of us who are now sixty-five and over were certainly not raised as feminists. Far from it. However, there is a new generation right behind us, and maybe we can stop for a minute and join them.

My daughter tells her husband, "We both work, dear heart. That means cooking and dishes and cleaning and taking out the garbage are as much your job as mine."

I expect him to laugh, or to ask her if she's lost her mind, but no, he smiles and says, "You're right. I agree with that."

My other daughter talks about how she and her husband share equally in all things. "It's one pot, and we both contribute and we both take." I remember getting one dollar a week personal allowance from my husband.

It brightens my day to listen to the young women. They have hyphenated married names, their own checking and savings accounts, cars in their names. And why not? If we're created equal, we're equal.

Most of us old ladies don't acquire this freedom until we're widowed and it's forced upon us. I never had a separate checking or savings account. I do now. I never bought a house or a car or insurance. I have done all of these things since my husband died. I ask myself now why it is that only through widowhood could I do any of these things? I knew women who had never learned to drive, had never tried to balance a checkbook. When their husbands died, they were lost souls.

I listen to some of my old lady friends whose husbands are still alive. The women are tired of cooking and cleaning, planning meals, shopping for food. After about meal number twenty-five thousand, the fun is gone. They resent cleaning toilets and scrubbing floors and dusting the furniture. Mostly they resent it because their retired husbands are relaxing in the big easy chair watching TV, or going out to golf with buddies, or hanging out at a favorite beer joint while they do these chores. The husband has worked for many years, and now he's retired and feels entitled to do as he pleases.

His wife has worked for many years, too. Sometimes in an outside job, sometimes not, but she has worked. When does her retirement come? Only when her husband dies? It appears so.

I have a friend who decided, after a few years of living with a retired husband, that she wasn't going to tolerate it anymore.

"I'm going to take care of myself," she told me. "I'm retired, too, and I want to enjoy my last years. I am just so sick and tired of doing the same old things that I've been doing for so many years, only now I have to walk around this retired husband, who sometimes sits in his pajamas in front of the TV all day.

I'm tired of having to ask him to lift his feet every time I vacuum!"

My friend wasn't particularly thinking about women's lib or feminism, she simply felt that it was time to think of herself.

I believe that one of a woman's most important duties is to develop all of her potential so that she can guide and teach the next generation. In order to do that, she has to consider herself equal with the rest of the population.

In biblical times the individuality of a woman was obliterated by marriage. We are emerging from that fog, thank God!

We old ladies aren't too concerned with women's lib. In many ways, the movement came too late for us to reap much of its benefits. However, there is still much we can do. We can applaud the young women and support them and cheer them on. Instead of sitting in criticism and muttering, "Well! That's not the way it was when I was young!" we can pat them on the back and say, "It's about time, sister!"

We can show them that their old age will probably be even better than ours because people are finally beginning to admit that women were created equal and should have equal rights with men. The sad thing is that it took centuries to recognize this truth. Teach the young women good things, and encourage them to share the same rights that men have enjoyed for so long. It's never too late to learn.

CHAPTER 5:

A Look at Ecclesiastes

There is one portion of Scripture that makes me chuckle. In Ecclesiastes the author describes old age and all that goes with it.

Of course, the aim of the author of Ecclesiastes was to show us that when we pursue earthly goals as ends in themselves, we only arrive at emptiness. Our highest goal should be in loving God and enjoying the gift of life as much as we possibly can.

When we reach the Ripened Age, we know the futility of striving after money and status; we know that beauty fades; we are reduced physically. Regardless of our material possessions, our status in society, our moments of fame, we all must arrive at the stage of ripened maturity. We might as well handle it with as much of a sense of humor as we can muster.

The alternative has been the subject of many jokes.

"I hate being old!"

"You should love it. Think of the alternative."

You know what the alternative is: death. Even though at times we may feel we would welcome the release of death, we can thank our God that the choice doesn't lie with us. Once that pain has been relieved, or that hurt forgotten, that slight forgiven, we are glad to be alive.

Most of the striving, pushing, and fighting of our youthful years is over now, and we can agree with the author of Ecclesiastes that it is all vanity. Because we wind up the same: old. And then dead.

Ecclesiastes 12:3 says:

In the day when the keepers of the house shall tremble, and the strong men shall bow themselves, and the grinders cease because they are few, and those that look out of the windows be darkened.

The keepers of the house are our hands and arms, and they do tremble because often they are weak. We get tired and forget to straighten our shoulders. We are thankful for dentists and denture products we can use to keep our teeth from flying out of our mouths when we laugh. We eat corn on the cob with the best of them. Sometimes we spend time searching for glasses that are perched on the top of our heads.

Verse 4:
And the doors shall be shut in the streets,

when the sound of the grinding is low, and he
shall rise up at the voice of the bird, and all
the daughters of music shall be brought low.

Here our doors are our ears, and sometimes it seems
that our doors have been slammed shut. We try to
avoid saying "Huh?" as much as possible. We don't
want to be stubborn old ladies refusing the wonders of
a hearing aid, but sometimes we are.

There are times when you can be glad you live
alone, and one of them is when you want to get up
at the sound of the first bird that chirps the breaking
of dawn. Young people sleep till the last possible moment, but we can't anymore. So when you wake up
and it's still dark and the world is asleep, get up and
enjoy the solitude. Commune with God in the quiet.
Remember to thank Him that you can't hear most of
the music the young people are playing.

Verse 5:
Also when they shall be afraid of that which
is high, and fears shall be in the way, and the
almond tree shall flourish, and the grasshopper
shall be a burden, and desire shall fail: because
man goeth to his long home, and the mourners
go about the streets.

Shortness of breath and our fear of heights can be
embarrassing! What we did so easily only a few years

ago now are little mountains to conquer. Our hair is white (or tinged with blue dye) like the almond tree in spring. I suppose we do look like a grasshopper dragging its legs. Sex? The fire may be in the furnace yet, but it's glowing embers now, not bursting into flame very often. The end will come and we will go home. Maybe many will mourn our leaving, maybe few, but it won't matter to us, will it?

You go through life being a daughter, wife, mother, grandmother. Maybe all of the above, maybe some of the above. It hasn't all been easy, but you are able to laugh and say, "Oh well, He never promised me a rose garden. With the help of God, I made it."

Of course you made it. You are an old lady, and you have seen a lot of changes—in your family, your friends, in you. You may barely have noted them at the time because you've been busy. After all, you have been leading an active, productive life.

Over the years you probably made some plans for your old age. You wanted there to be enough money and a place to live and something to do. In the meantime, you have been needed for so many things and by so many people. Once in a while you thought about the retirement years, the so-called Golden Age, but it was always a distant contemplation of a time that was somewhere down the road.

• And then your dear husband of so many years dies. This was not what the two of you had planned.

• The children leave. And it's not only your tuna casserole they don't need anymore, but also your advice and your presence. They are busy cutting the apron strings, and you had no idea it would hurt so much.

• You experience a devastating and frightening loneliness. You never dreamed you would sit in a corner and feel so sorry for yourself!

• Some of your friends die.

• You give up trying to count the wrinkles.

• You have snapshots that testify to your youthful beauty. You look in the mirror and ask, "What happened?"

• Where in the world do all the little aches and pains come from?

• Your hair is gray and going white, and you have finally given up on the rinses and dyes. Now it's getting thin on top.

• You have to face it: You're old, and there is more time behind you than there is ahead of you.

On my fortieth birthday I got my first pair of glasses. I cried. It seemed to me that I was beginning to fall apart. Then I sailed through my fiftieth birthday because I felt great. I was working full-time, as I had been for years, and people told me that they couldn't believe I was fifty. "You certainly don't look it or act it," they said.

No one says that anymore. I tell people that I am sixty-eight and they say, "Oh."

My grown children love me and are good to me, but they really don't need me. They are busy living their lives, pursuing their dreams, very much self-centered. This is right and good. I try very hard not to feel abandoned and neglected and sorry for myself.

My husband died over twenty years ago, and I still miss him with an ache that won't go away. It never will. Assuring myself that we will one day meet in heaven doesn't ease the pain.

I have had a lot of friends in my years of life. Some are dead, many have drifted away, a few are "letters only" friends now because great distances separate us.

There are so many things I can't do anymore! I never felt restricted before. I can't wear my hair long because that looks silly on an old lady. I could twist it up in a bun on top of my head, but I can't seem to manage that with style. Speaking of style, I can't wear most of the latest dresses. I don't think many of the current fashions look all that great on the young, but that's another story.

For so many years I didn't have time to watch television. I called it a vast wasteland and was a little proud that I had never become addicted to it. Now TV is a sort of blessing. It fills many lonely hours. It is the sound of a voice in my house.

A portrait of an old lady? Sure! Typical? Of course!

My problem is that I don't want to be a typical

old lady. I want better. I am a Christian old lady, and this should make a difference, shouldn't it?

In all situations I look for ways in which I can show that, because I am a Christian, I am not a typical old lady.

Of course, anyone can be old and complaining and lonely and defeated by age. That's easy. Just sit back and let it happen and feel sorry for yourself. You will be able to hear yourself rusting away.

It requires courage to be something other than that. Old age is not for cowards. It takes tremendous stamina to be a woman of faith. Now is your chance to show that what you believed in for so long is true.

You can be a happy old lady. Alone maybe, but you don't have to dwell on your loneliness. You can appreciate every day that you're alive. You can look back on your tender memories with joy and look forward to what's left with the same joy. A woman of faith has to be different from a woman of no faith, or her convictions have all been meaningless.

For years you have professed faith in God. You taught your children that faith and hoped it would give them the strength and comfort it has given you. Now you are old and nobody needs you, and you're not exactly thrilled about the prospect of maybe fifteen or twenty more years of this.

At one point I asked myself: "Is this all there is? After such a full life, am I going to be dumped until

I die? What if I live to be seventy-five? Or eighty-five? That's a long time to be a dumpee!"

Let me tell you, I nearly went crazy thinking about that!

However, I found some answers that changed my life. Considerably. Read on, dear old lady. Maybe there will be an answer or two for you, too.

Getting Personal: Be Good to Yourself; You're Worth It

CHAPTER 6:

You Are Not a Nobody

I have heard about famous people mingling in a crowd with other celebrities and a fan coming up to them with autograph book in hand.

"Are you anybody?" they ask.

Implying, I suppose, that if the person isn't a star, he isn't anybody. He is a nobody.

Who are you? Are you anybody? The world tells us in no uncertain terms that we don't amount to much if we don't possess money, power, or fame. Or, most important, youth. I don't have an abundance of any of those things. Does that mean I'm a nobody?

I don't care. All I want is security and comfort and a measure of peace. I never thought much about those particular conditions until I grew old. When I was young and ambitious, I didn't spend much time worrying about my tomorrows. I had my hands full taking care of the todays.

Now there are times when I desperately need to believe that tomorrow is going to take care of itself, as the Bible says. Too often I feel helpless and very much alone and a nobody. In the Bible I read: "Take therefore no thought for the morrow: for the morrow shall take thought for the things of itself. Sufficient unto the day is the evil thereof." (Matthew 6:34)

Okay! Those are comforting words, and I really want to live my life believing that I don't have to worry about tomorrow. I want to believe that I am somebody no matter what the world says. Still, I observe the world around me, and it's not easy to surrender anxiety.

I was a SPAR (U.S. Coast Guard) during World War II. One of my brothers was killed in that war, and another one saw such horrors, it was a miracle his mind didn't self-destruct. We loved our country and we were willing to work and make sacrifices for it. I know that I prayed very hard for peace.

To say that I am disappointed isn't nearly half of what I feel. I feel beaten down, black and blue in my soul. Sometimes I feel like a foolish old woman looking out at a world that has gone crazy. I feel very much like a nobody. Nothing has changed because of the bright, eager, patriotic things any of us did. It has all become tarnished.

I remember the lump in my throat when the American flag passed me in a parade. I had such sweet, high hopes for my country. We would beat the enemy! We would be victorious!

We beat the enemy, all right. We won the war.

But I sit here in my old age, and it looks as though we are decaying from within. It is terrible to feel that nothing you ever did meant anything. Talk about being a nobody! The young world of today looks at me and says, "Poor old fuddy-duddy!"

I need to feel that I am somebody. I don't have much money, and it's a constant, nagging worry that the day will come when I will have to depend on my children to take care of me. Would plenty of money make me somebody?

Fame has managed to elude me all my life. Oh, once after just having a book published, the publishers sent me to a big department store for an autographing party. Fame at last! But I was seated at a card table behind a stack of my books, and very few people even saw me. The store clerks ignored me completely. A handful of people found me and asked if my book was in the library. We sold one autographed copy of my book that day. Fame wasn't what it was cracked up to be after all.

I certainly don't wield any power over anyone. I used to have power over my children. I was the one who decided when and what they would eat and wear. I told them when to cross the street. That power has long since faded into a dim memory. I don't have any power in the commercial world. If I should want to buy a car, I wouldn't think of trying to do it alone. I would ask a man to go with me because he would have the power to wheel and deal, regardless of the fact that he may be less smart than me. I can guess what they think when they see one old lady walking into the car lot: a sitting duck!

Youth automatically makes you somebody. Most of the advertisers cater to youth. The manufacturers of practically everything depend on the whims and fads and tastes of youth. TV, movies, and books are primarily about or directed to youth. My youth is gone. For a few years I frequently traveled cross-country to present seminars. I ran alone through airports, lugging my luggage. Then my young, pretty daughter accompanied me on one of my trips, and my eyes were opened. I can't begin to count the number of offers she received to carry her luggage. I trudged along behind her, mumbling about how young and strong she was and how she didn't need to have her luggage carried, but as long as I didn't faint dead away, I received no offers of help.

So what does that make me? Besides an old lady, am I anybody?

I slogged through a dark valley for a while and almost reached the point where I wondered if life was worth the effort. I seriously doubted it. However, I am thankful for a faith that lifts me up even out of those valleys.

God tells us to stop worrying. We don't have to feel that we are nobody and that there is nothing we can do about anything.

"I am still in charge," God assures us through His

word. "I love you," He says, "and as far as I am concerned, you are somebody. Tomorrow will take care of itself. I know what is down the road, and I am in command. Be at peace."

And that's all we can do. Take Him at His word.

An old lady friend of mine called the other day. "Jane, don't you think that God is looking at us and crying?" she asked.

I don't know. Perhaps. The fact that I hold dear is that He loves all of us; each of us is precious to Him, and He is in charge. I really don't have to do anything but be at peace with that truth.

And to know that as far as God is concerned, I am somebody.

I can be somebody in other ways, too. Once in a while my daughter calls. "Mama, I just have to unload." So she talks for an hour, and I listen and sympathize and let her know how much I love her. She lives far away and has a good husband who loves her, but I can still be somebody who listens and understands.

I'm somebody to my friends. Sometimes I am a special somebody when I am able to help them, but most of the time I'm somebody who is always glad to see them.

I have other friends who live far away. To them, I am somebody who writes and keeps long-standing ties from breaking.

Almost everyone, young and old, can feel like a

nobody. To the doctor, you are just a patient; to the grocer, a customer; to the lawyer, a client. You need to feel that you are important in a personal way to someone. If you are old and alone, you need it more than ever. Begin with the assurance that you are important to God, and let that give you confidence. Then branch out to family and friends and build your importance here and there in small ways.

Take your family, one by one. Try to figure out ways in which you can be more important to them. Think of something besides just the fact of your existence and what you have done for them in the past.

Perhaps a daughter would really get a kick out of receiving snapshots of your bird-watching trips;

Or a son would welcome a batch of your cookies on a regular basis;

Or a friend would be overjoyed if you phoned now and then.

Think of things to do. Not earthshaking things, just little, friendly, caring things. You will probably be surprised at the results.

I read about a woman who made arrangements with a fried chicken place and had chicken dinners sent to a retirement home one evening. Another had pizzas delivered once every other month. Depending on your financial circumstances, this is a marvelous way to spread happiness. Perhaps you and some of your friends could do this together. If you can't afford chicken or pizza, a couple of your special cakes or pies would be welcome.

I remember one time moaning and groaning because my house needed cleaning and I wasn't up to the job. A friend said, "Let's do it together," and we did. We took a whole week to do it and it was fun. You may know someone who would be very happy if you offered to clean house with her.

Every time you go to the store, stop and think. Is there someone you can call to see if they need anything or if they would like to go with you? I recall doing this one time and I was amazed. The lady said that she had everything she needed, except for a fresh head of lettuce. "I haven't had a salad for a week!"

One woman makes simple, flowing mu-mu's for casual summer wear. She is always on the lookout for sales of bright cotton material and she gives these mu-mu's to friends who don't sew.

I have a friend who every now and then calls me and says, "Let's go to the beach and stare at the ocean." Those quiet, staring times are some of the happiest moments of my life. You don't have to invite a friend to go to a concert or a movie. Maybe just a quiet walk, a time of being together and staring at something is all that is needed.

All kinds of little tragedies enter people's lives almost on a daily basis. Stay alert and watch for opportunities to help. A friend told me: "Jane, when I'm hurting you always climb right down into the hole with me." Yes, I do. I feel her pain and I cry with her and then, together, we climb out and try to figure out how we can make the situation better.

My son-in-law popped in unexpectedly one day and said, "I figured you might need a hug." That kept me floating a few inches off the ground for several days! Is there someone you know who would appreciate a hug?

I once heard an old lady say, "Why, my daughter simply couldn't make it through the month unless I sent over one of my coffee cakes."

At the time, I thought that old lady was a silly dreamer, but now I'm not so sure. When you give of yourself, you really are somebody.

CHAPTER 7:

Try New Challenges

It's easy to fall into a rut, decide it's comfortable, and stay there. Don't do it! It can be devastating. There are simple ways to rust-proof yourself. If I were a young person, I would probably tell you to get up and jog or ride a bike or find a job. But I am an old lady like you, and I have more practical advice.

You don't have to do mind-boggling things, or become famous, or act foolish. You only have to dream a little, think about things you have always wanted to do but never had the time for. Explore new possibilities, take on a few new challenges.

Start a diary. Describe the weather as it looks from your window, write about your memories and your friends and the things you are doing. The art of diary keeping is almost lost; you can help to keep it alive. It can be a part of you to leave for your children.

Flash is teaching my daughter how to tat, to make lace, and there aren't many people who know this craft. It should not be forgotten.

I make old lady apple heads. Here's how you do it: Peel an apple and cut the bottom so it will sit straight. With a sharp stick or pencil, make holes for eyes, carve a nose and a mouth. Put cloves or round allspice in the holes for eyes. Then lightly carve some downward lines around the corners of the mouth and some wrinkles on the cheeks and across the forehead. If you can spare a little hair off your head, cut it and glue it on top of the apple. Then watch your old lady age. Day by day her wrinkles will deepen and she will shrivel.

You can make one or you can have a whole lineup of them on a windowsill. You can stick the head on top of a bottle and make a dress or a shawl to cover the bottle.

If anyone asks you what you're doing, tell them, "I just like to see something besides myself grow old!"

If you believe you're too old to try something new, then you are. Don't forget, you can get away with a lot of things now that you wouldn't dare try when you were young and cared a great deal about what others thought of you. You know by now that others aren't paying that much attention to what you do.

Take the subject of eating out. One of the frustrations of my life was that throughout our marriage, my husband and I couldn't afford to eat out, except on rare occasions. Even when we could afford it, my dear husband preferred to come home to my cooking.

I couldn't blame him for that, but I nagged often enough that we ate out sporadically.

Now here I am, alone, and I can do pretty much as I please. Right? Nope! How do you feel about going to a nice restaurant alone? It's the pits!

However, I was lucky. When I was traveling all over the country, conducting seminars, I always ordered room service for my evening meal. Or I bought bags of snack items from machines in the motel lobby. Or I packed a jar of instant coffee and granola bars in my suitcase.

I got tired of those meals, but entering a restaurant alone and facing a waiter and the couples at tables took more courage than I had.

Eventually I got so bored with chewing on dry stuff in my room that I mustered up some courage from somewhere inside. I made sure that I looked presentable and then I went to the dining room of the hotel. Inside I told the maitre d', "I'm alone. I would like a table by the window, please."

My theory was: Don't go in meek and mild, grateful for any bone they toss my way.

It worked. I was escorted to a table by the window, and when the waiter came I told him that I was dining alone and that I would like a cup of coffee before I ordered. I received excellent service, and I never again ate granola bars in my hotel room. In fact, I grew so bold that in some towns I found out about unusual restaurants and drove to them for my evening meal.

You can do this in your own town. The point is, if you want to eat out, do it. It can be extremely pleasant. Get dressed up and visit any restaurant that pleases you. Don't take a book to read. Look around and smile and enjoy your meal. Talk to your waitress or waiter. Learn his or her name. If you are given good service, leave a generous tip. The next time you go to that restaurant, ask for that waitress or waiter by name. You will be welcomed and will continue to be treated like a preferred customer. Try it!

Every once in a while (not every day) ask yourself: "What can I do today that's different?" It doesn't have to be some big, earthshaking accomplishment. But it should be something you haven't ever done but always wanted to do, or something you enjoy doing but hardly ever do. Shake up your routine every now and then. It will help to keep that rust from forming.

Think of all the things you really enjoy doing and the things you once did. Write them down. Think of all the things you are really good at doing. Write them down.

Your list might look something like this:
- Dancing
- Singing in a choir or group
- Taking pictures
- Drawing/painting
- Writing (fiction, nonfiction, poetry)
- Giving perms; cutting/setting hair

- Making Christmas ornaments
- Decorating elaborate Easter eggs
- Playing a musical instrument
- Knitting

The list can take quite a long time to complete. You have to search your memory and pull out half-forgotten talents and activities you enjoyed and were accomplished at. Next you have to decide whether or not you would like to try to do these things now that you have time. (Remember, your age is no excuse for doing nothing!)

Take the first item on my list, for example: dancing. When I was young I loved to dance, and I was a sought-after partner. In my day, the jitterbug was the fad, and it was intricate. You had to concentrate to learn the steps. It was great exercise, too. I recalled how much I loved to dance, the fact that it involves other people, but believe me, jitterbugging is out of the question now. Nobody does that anymore, anyway. Still, I didn't cross dancing off my list. Then one day I read about a square-dancing group. Singles welcome. Full skirts with voluminous petticoats. It appealed to me, and when I saw a picture in the paper of a local square-dancing group of my generation, I decided to leave dancing on my list. I haven't joined the group yet because I believe that joining anything must involve commitment, and I'm not quite ready, but it is one of the things I look forward to doing.

Nearly all of the things on your list will necessitate your leaving the house and making contact with other people. Joining a church choir, for example, will mean one night for rehearsal and Sunday-morning attendance. You will be doing something you enjoy, making a contribution, and being a part of a group.

Some of the things on your list will be lonely occupations, but if it is what pleases you and stimulates you, go for it.

Visualize a typical day, from the time you awake until you go to bed. What pleased you the most? (Taking care of your house plants, talking on the phone, making cookies, visiting with a neighbor, sewing, etc.) Don't think about the things you did that pleased you the least. They don't belong on your list.

Think about it. Are there places and people who would benefit or gain some pleasure if you did one or more of these things for them? Just about any place with children would welcome homemade cookies; many communities need volunteers for hot lines; your expertise with house plants could be shared in a lecture at the local library.

Compile your list and then search your newspaper. Try to match your skills with the needs in the paper. Don't be afraid to pick up the phone and volunteer. Get your name on some lists. If they don't need you now, they probably will later.

This list making can take several days or weeks, but eventually you will have it all written down. Go through your list and see if there is any reason why you can't do these things. (I said reason, not an excuse!)

Be experimental; have an open mind. You may eventually scratch a few items off your list, for various legitimate reasons, but remember, there is one excuse that is not acceptable: "I'm too old."

For instance, I had been reading about how good exercise is for you, how it's important at any age. I lead a very sedentary life, and I knew that this was something I should try. I ordered a stationary bicycle, and it arrived in pieces with instructions on how to assemble it. In less than a week I called the store and told them to pick up their pieces. Obviously, this was not the solution.

I knew the one exercise I could do and would enjoy was walking, but I was afraid. I was afraid to leave my apartment and walk. I told myself that I would look silly. I convinced myself that there were any number of strange men out there waiting for the chance to rape me. It took weeks for me to build up enough confidence to walk out of my apartment and once around the block. No one laughed at me, no one raped me, and I felt wonderful. I have lost weight and my legs are stronger, and since I live in a community of older people, I meet and greet the regular walkers every morning.

You may be thinking: She dashed all over the country giving seminars, and now she's trying to tell me that she was afraid to go outside her apartment and take a walk?

Let me tell you something: I read somewhere that a person changes drastically every seven years. I believe it. Compare a newborn to a seven-year-old; a seven-year-old to a fourteen-year-old, and so on. I dashed through airports, drove rented cars in strange places in pouring rain; I arrived at motels after midnight, praying they had held my room. (One time they didn't, and I spent the night fully clothed, scared to death, on a cot in the motel's laundry room.) Yes, I conducted seminars for over two years, but I honestly believe that I hit one of those seven-year changes between the end of the seminars and my move to an apartment. Suddenly I had fears I had never before experienced. However, we must never allow our fears to overwhelm us. Okay, so I had taken one of those seven-year nosedives. Now I had to do something about it. In my case, I had to get myself out of my apartment and take a walk. When we acknowledge our fears, we can conquer them. The worst thing is to give in to them.

I'm sure this sounds strange to a young person. Imagine being afraid to take a walk! Still, it was true. We may have to psych ourselves into doing any number of things, but success is rewarding.

In the subtropical climate where I live, brisk walking outdoors in summer is risky, so I march briskly around my air-conditioned apartment. We can't allow ourselves any excuses, or we quickly sink back into apathy.

You may be amazed at the new things you can try, at the fun you can have. Study your list from time to time and let new ideas come to you.

One old lady wrote on her list that she was a very good seamstress. She enjoyed making all of her summer cotton dresses and nightgowns. One day she was telling someone about this work, and the person asked her if she would make a dress for her little girl. The lady paid for the pattern, the material, and extra for the labor.

Now our old lady has to turn people down! Word got around, and busy working mothers and career women beat a path to her door. She accepts only the work she wants to do and no more. The money she's earning she is saving for a vacation.

It really doesn't take much to haul yourself out of a rut.

I remember my mother telling me that she had always thought she would be adept with a Hula Hoop. (Remember those?) She was an old lady, but I got her a Hula Hoop and she spent days trying to master it. She was proud of the fact that she was better at it than some of the kids in the neighborhood.

Another old lady regretted the fact that she had never learned to ride a bike. So, with some guiding help from her friends, she set out to learn. The first day she actually landed bottom-up in a pile of trash.

But I can look out the window today and see her with a big smile covering her face, bicycling down the street.

A rut is a very dull, confining place to live. It's sort of like a coffin. If you're in one, don't stay there. Get out your dreams and make some of them come true.

CHAPTER 8:

Be Honest with Yourself

I have lived long enough not to believe everything I hear.

Someone says to me, "Oh, I go to church every Sunday. I love the dear Lord so much!"

One woman told me that God talks to her almost on a daily basis. He tells her what to do and what not to do.

Another old lady insists that all she wants to do is to live a life pleasing to the Lord.

I can't help it. I say to myself, "Prove it, lady!"

Over the years I have listened to these marvelous, religious statements and affirmations so often. People tell me how much they love the Lord, how close to God they are, how saintly they strive to be.

And yet I have seen these same people withhold their love, knowing how much it hurt someone else; they have criticized others without knowing complete details and withheld their precious dollars even though they knew the money would buy food for starving children. They have sailed self-righteously through life, leaving a trail of hurt, puzzled, and sometimes broken hearts. I have been guilty of some of these unlovely acts, too.

It reminds me of the people who say they want to be writers. I finally have that figured out, too. They want to be writers, but they don't want to write.

Writing is extremely hard work and requires an amazing amount of self-discipline. There is nothing easy or glamorous about it. You have to brace yourself for rejection, and it's a lonely occupation. It doesn't even have the virtue of using up calories.

A few years ago, after having a dozen or so books published, I decided that since God had blessed me with some talent, I should share that gift with struggling would-be writers.

I believe that, except in the case of the rare genius, artistic success is composed of one golden drop of God-given talent and ninety-nine percent hard work. I was more than willing to share what I had learned with anyone who had that drop of talent and was willing to work.

After six people had asked for my help, I discovered that none of them was willing to expend the ninety-nine percent energy. They just wanted to cash in. They did not want to work. Not one of them.

Some of us want to be known as moral, upright people, but we don't want to work at it. The adage,

"Talk is cheap" is true. You have to prove that you mean what you say or else stop saying it.

Take the old lady who was in one of my Bible study classes. For some reason, she liked to talk about the lack of morals of young women today. In any discussion she never failed to mention sex and young women and how terrible they were. She also added that she tried to be pure in mind and deed and didn't know why all women couldn't be like her.

I angered her one day. "I'm sure you haven't indulged in any sinful sexual activities," I remarked.

She nodded vigorously and self-righteously.

"Tell me. When was the last time you had an opportunity to indulge in sinful sexual activity?"

It was cruel, I know, but I was really asking her to prove what she was bragging about.

If men had been pursuing her, begging her for sexual favors, and if she was tempted to give in but refused on moral grounds, then I would applaud her.

But if no man had asked her for years, and if her own sexual appetite had faded long ago, why was she blowing her own horn?

Should I boast about not drinking a glass of whiskey in over half a century? I hate the smell and taste of whiskey.

Old ladies bragging about what they don't do, attaching moral purity to their abstinence, are pitiful. Who cares what you don't do?

Quite a few years ago, when I was a fairly young widow, I met a woman in a Laundromat. She was about my age, and we chatted while our clothes tumbled around in the dryers.

She talked about going to singles bars and picking up men and going home with them. She invited me to go with her one night.

I told her I wasn't interested in that sort of thing.

"What do you do about guys?" she asked.

"I don't do anything. I have four children to raise. That's a big enough job for me. There isn't time for anything else."

"Are you trying to tell me that there is no sex in your life?"

She couldn't believe that I was for real. Our conversation disintegrated after that. I suppose she left the Laundromat thinking I was some kind of self-righteous religious freak. I know that I left thinking she was a slut.

Still, memories of that encounter bother me to this day. She had been willing to prove that her way of life was okay. She invited me to go to a singles bar with her. If I recall correctly, she offered to pick me up and take me.

But I hadn't been willing to offer proof that my way was the right way. I didn't try to convince her. I didn't invite her to my church or to my home.

Not that she would have accepted, I suppose, but the point is, I didn't even try. I sat next to her, mentally labeling her a slut, feeling very superior and pious. But I did absolutely nothing to try and prove to her why I believed the way I did.

We become smug the older we get. We may have "raised some hell" in our youth, but now old age covers our sins, and boy, are we saintly. Let's face it. We no longer have the desire or opportunity to do sinful things; we know that some vices lead to unhappiness; we know that some are harmful and just plain foolish. But that knowledge doesn't give us the right to condemn all the young people who are rushing headlong into life and all the goodies that await them. If you profess to be a Christian, then prove it.

We are supposed to love with patience. To be kind. We are not to brag about how good we are. We are not to be easily angered, and we don't keep a record of everyone else's sins. We protect and trust and hope and persevere. (Read I Corinthians 13:1–13.)

We old ladies are not to sit up there on our thrones of goodness and self-righteousness and condemn the young. We are to teach them good things.

Also, no matter what we think about the morals of young people today, there is always hope. Joshua 6:17 tells the story of a harlot, Rahab. What counted was not what she was but what she became.

Throughout the Bible we learn of people in desperate search for God. Many were far from perfect but rose up out of their sinfulness to become people of God.

Even at our age we are not hopeless. We have time to verify all our lovely talk about faith and goodness. We can start by refusing to turn up our noses at those who don't live their lives as we do. And we can start by being honest with ourselves.

There is a saying about old age: If you want to be a loving, gentle, kind old person, you had better start practicing now. Although this advice is directed to the young, it's not too late to start practicing. Because all you're going to get from here on in is older. But there is still hope!

CHAPTER 9:

Live Your Life as It Pleases You

When I visit my friend Flash, we are like two old shoes. We have known each other for so many years that all pretenses have dissolved. Two old shoes: a little worn, but comfortable.

Still, when we drink coffee, Flash serves it in translucent bone china cups. On the table is an exquisite handmade cloth with matching napkins.

For lunch we may have a plate of steamed vegetables. Nothing fancy, but the vegetables are arranged artistically on a beautiful old platter.

We sip and dine like ladies. First class all the way.

So what? Does it really matter whether you drink from a china cup or a coffee mug? Or if the napkins are cloth or paper?

Maybe it does. Especially as we grow older. Because these little things can show how we feel about ourselves.

How many of you have silver coffee sets, exquisite china, and lovely hand-sewn linen? Where are they?

Enfolded in plastic? Wrapped in blue paper? Stowed away in drawers? Why? So they will be in perfect condition for your heirs? Heirs who probably won't care a fig about them.

When my husband and I were young we visited another young couple. He was a doctor and she was an artist. My husband was a pastor, and in those days pastors' wives didn't do unorthodox things. They were very careful about how they dressed and talked and acted. I can still recall the distress I felt on entering a local woman's club meeting. The ladies were in small groups, talking and laughing and having a great old time. When I entered the room, the gaiety had a lid put on it. Voices stilled, the laughter faded. They started talking about God. I had so wanted to join the fun and instead stopped it.

Anyway, my husband and I visited this young doctor and his artist wife, and I stepped into a world that brought on a severe attack of envy.

We had been invited to dinner. Before dinner, our hostess brought out a wooden cutting board. On it were some hunks of cheese, crackers, and a couple of knives.

We sat on the floor, around the coffee table, and nibbled on cheese and crackers and enjoyed the most marvelous conversation. Not one word about God.

Later, her husband had to send out for pizza because she forgot all about the roast in the oven.

In her dining room all the furniture had been shoved against one wall to make room for two easels. She needed extra space to teach her little son how to paint.

My restricted life was like a bite of meat caught in my throat. I envied this woman and her freedom to be herself.

Imagine a pastor's wife making you sit on the floor, eating hunks of cheese off a cutting board! And burning dinner because she was talking! Today it could happen. But thirty or forty years ago? No way!

After my husband's death, and after the kids were gone, I did a turnaround. I still remembered that free soul from years ago, and I resolved, "I am going to be like that. Now I can do it."

It didn't work. I didn't want to serve cheese on a cutting board, or sit on the floor and not care if I burned dinner. I wanted to go first class, the way Flash did.

There is another side to this. I know many old ladies who own silver coffee and tea sets, lovely linen, glassware, and dishes. They might polish them and use them for a holiday meal or a very special occasion, but otherwise these lovely pieces stay hidden in their protective wrappings.

"I'm glad I had these things," they say. "During my entertaining years they were a definite asset. Now, because they must be polished and washed and cared for, they are a liability. I could display them, but why? So that people who come to my home will be made aware of the fact that I own these things? Who cares?"

The point is, we change. Our circumstances change, and things we once felt were important aren't any longer. Accept the changes, and do what pleases you. Travel the way you want to travel. You can afford to indulge yourself, and you should.

After all these years, I can be myself. I can do what I enjoy doing and do it the way I want to do it.

I started collecting pictures of clowns. One wall of my study is covered with pictures of clowns—photos, paintings, and some needlepoint. People ask, "Why are you so interested in clowns?"

I once saw a picture of a clown sitting cross-legged in front of a crucifix. Tears glistened in his eyes. That got me started.

Come into my home, ask me about clowns, and we'll have a good hour of delightful conversation ahead of us. I have studied the history and ministry of clowns, and I have a number of lovely little stories to tell about them.

It beats talking about how terribly lonely I am. Or about how my kids ignore me. How my health isn't as good as it used to be. The only thing is, before I would never have done anything so silly as to collect clowns. Now I do it because it pleases me.

I talked to a woman once who told me that before her husband died, she had never lived one day of her life alone. "It has been the most unbearable thing I have ever experienced," she said. "Sometimes I think I am going out of my mind with loneliness."

I feel very sorry for that poor woman, but I can do little for her. I can't move in with her and keep her company.

I had never lived alone, either. I was raised in a large family, I had seven roommates in the SPARS, I married and had a houseful of kids. Eventually everybody left, one way or another, and I discovered loneliness in my old age.

I don't know the statistics, but I would bet that loneliness tops the list of the "worsts" of old age.

Yes, it is devastating. It does make you feel sometimes that you might go out of your mind.

But what is loneliness? It's a big, empty space that others used to keep filled. Now they're gone, so you have to fill up the space with something else. In a way, loneliness is a form of self-indulgence.

I love to stay home usually. The silence doesn't bother me at all. Yet every once in a while it gets to me. I know it's a danger sign when I start meeting myself around the corner. It won't be too long before I will dissolve into self-pity.

So I go to the shopping mall. I ask the clerks questions that have to be answered. I talk to strangers and I pat small children on the head.

Then I come home reeling with the sounds of people, and I am content to be alone for a while.

Sometimes, calling someone will dispel the emptiness, or going next door to see how a neighbor is doing. Maybe just taking a walk and listening to the sounds of nature will be enough.

Whatever it is that pleases you, that keeps you from climbing the walls or screaming, do it. When you live like this, you're going first class.

Make your life and yourself interesting. When people come to visit, give them something to talk about. It may be coffee served in your best china cups; or your apple lady's progress; or it may be chunks of cheese served on a cutting board. Going first class doesn't involve money. First class is being alive and interested and different from anyone else.

CHAPTER 10:

Develop the Habit of Hope

I remember an old lady who gave up hope. I watched her, day after day, allow the hope to slip away from her until she disintegrated. She sank down into herself. She lost weight, and the doctors didn't know why. She became lethargic. She no longer cared about anything or anyone. You could see it in her eyes.

I went to her home and was appalled. This once neat, clean lady was grimy. Her clothes were wrinkled and stained. Food rotted in ugly little clumps in her refrigerator. Cobwebs decorated the corners and ceilings.

Nothing was physically wrong with her. The doctors said so. But she died.

Her son had been sent to prison for armed robbery, and her daughter was living with a man who was little more than a bum. So she gave up hope and died.

I felt sorry for her. It's tough when your children stomp on your heart like that. But she was weak. She had nothing in her life that she cared about but her children. She had failed to fill the gaps they left in her life.

You can't fight some things. But you can accept them. You can tell yourself, "All right, this is rough. But I have been through rough times before. I'll make it!" Hope in your heart will keep you alive.

That woman could have thought about what she could do for her son. She could have written to him, visited him, let him know that in spite of what he had done, she loved him. It might have made a big difference in his life. She might have been his salvation.

She could have let her daughter know that even though she did not approve of her living situation, her mother loved her and would always be there for her. In a quiet way, she could have taught her daughter good things.

We read news items all the time of people who cling to life against all odds. They continue living long after the doctors say they should be dead. These people harbor hope, and strong hope brings about psychological and physiological changes that strengthen the body's resistance.

In my youth I was plagued with migraine headaches. Their severity eased as I grew older, but I was still subject to tension headaches. Yet with hope, which is nothing more than a positive attitude, I have vanished headaches from my life. I haven't taken any medication for years. And I have never allowed a headache to gain the tiniest foothold. I can attest to the fact that a positive attitude can affect your physical self.

If you can change the circumstances that have left you desolate, get busy and do something.

If you can't change anything, then hope. It is a passive way of coping with what you absolutely can't do anything about. It's healthful.

Resolve to maintain a positive outlook. Make it a habit to sustain hope in your heart. Hope tells you that everything is going to be okay, that you will be able to cope with the low blows life hands you. It is not a Pollyanna attitude, but simply a denial that life can ever pull you down. Cling to this attitude; it could save your life somewhere down the road.

My son rode a bus from Chicago to Corpus Christi. At the end of the trip he exclaimed, "I love Texas! Even their road signs are great." He said that all the way from Chicago he saw signs that read, Stop! and Don't Enter and Wrong Way.

Upon entering Texas he saw signs that read, Drive Friendly and Ease On Down the Road.

"I sure do like that positive attitude," he said.

A positive attitude will help you cope with life more than you can imagine. The tone of your voice, the smile on your face, your enthusiasm all tell others that you are a person with hope. It tells your body not to give up.

Live your life with gusto and joy. Talk about the good things that happen. Let people know that you love them and appreciate them. It all bounces back on you and keeps you happy.

I know an old lady who sprained her ankle and had to go to a doctor. While she was in the office, he asked her when she had had her last checkup.

"About twenty years ago," she told him.

He was shocked and asked why she hadn't seen a doctor since then.

"Because I haven't needed a doctor," she replied.

He insisted that she have a complete physical immediately.

Later, he told her that she was fine. "For your age, you are in almost perfect health."

She just smiled, "I know."

Doctors admit that a large percentage of their patients suffer from imagined ailments. Burdened with negative attitudes, they are sure something is wrong with them when there isn't.

I know people who run to doctors regularly. It's almost as if they won't be satisfied until one of the doctors finds something wrong.

I don't mean that no one should ever visit a doctor. I believe in doctors. But why pay them money and take up their valuable time when there is nothing wrong with you? If it ain't broke, why fix it?

I know women who are addicted to Valium. "My nerves are shot," they say. Some pop all kinds of medication into their mouths on a daily basis.

What nonsense!

A newspaper reported about a woman whose son was pinned beneath a car. She lifted the car so that he could crawl out to safety. "I never dreamed I had that much strength," she said.

That woman was highly motivated. You can be just as highly motivated if you consider that your attitude can save your life.

The Bible tells us:

> For verily I say unto you, that whosoever shall say unto this mountain, Be thou removed, and be thou cast into the sea; and shall not doubt in his heart, but shall believe that those things which he saith shall come to pass; he shall have whatsoever he saith. Therefore I say unto you, what things soever ye desire, when ye pray, believe that ye receive them, and ye shall have them. (Mark 11:23–24)

What powerful words! Nurture a positive attitude. Believe. Don't neglect prayer.

And then let yourself be amazed at the change in your life.

CHAPTER 11:

Work Toward a Better You

Some women spend most of their time moaning and groaning because they so seldom see their grandchildren.

"They live so far away, and I never see my little darlings!"

"Those poor children are growing up barely knowing what their Grandma looks like!"

"It's just not fair!"

Have you ever been guilty of talking like that? I have. When I talk on the phone to my faraway grandson, I laugh and say, "Howdy, y'all!" so that he will know it's his grandma in Texas. Deep down, of course, I resent having to identify myself.

What we're doing is groping around in the past. We remember those wonderful, happy years when we cooked for the family and were surrounded by the noise and laughter of children. It was such a beautiful time of our lives (especially in retrospect), and we yearn to recapture it.

Be careful what you wish for: you may get it. What if, for any number of reasons, your grandchildren came to live with you? Think about it. I guarantee it wouldn't take long for you to go crazy. The noise children make will do it. And you are no longer used to cooking three big meals a day and keeping the jar stocked with homemade cookies. You will miss your quiet afternoon naps and having the TV to yourself.

We cannot bring back the past, which is probably for the best.

True, there are large gaps in our lives. A husband dies, the children leave home, and we're alone. We cry about those gaps, but what we must do is fill them, not cry and feel sorry for ourselves because of them. Life is never going to be the way it used to be, and we should probably be thanking God for that!

We must fill those gaps with things that are pleasant for us, perhaps productive, just so we fill them before someone decides to do it for us.

My twenty-seven-year-old son was between jobs recently and stayed with me for a few weeks. At first, I was so happy I nearly exploded. Just like old times! I cooked and baked and felt alive. That lasted for almost a week. Then I realized that I had forgotten how much food young men can put away, and I got very tired of planning meals, shopping, cooking, and cleaning up afterward. He didn't care for any of my favorite TV shows; he came in late at night and I worried. He was very noisy, and I thought he drank too much. I loved him with all my heart, but I kept wondering when he was going to leave. One night he said to me, "Mom, you're getting hostile!" I guess I was, and it saddened me a little, but the truth was, he belonged in his world and I belonged in mine. The long-ago days when I fed him and took care of him were gone, and there was no way we could recapture them.

Of course, we remember the past and like to look at our photo albums and sometimes talk about our yesterdays. There is nothing wrong with this, even if young people seldom understand why we do it. However, it's not where we were that's important, or even where we are. It's where we're going, what we're going to do with the years still left, that should occupy our minds. How are we going to fill in the gaps once occupied by children and mate? We can't fill those gaps with the same people or the same experiences, and we shouldn't try. We must fill them with new people, experiences, and interests that please us and make us happy.

Recently my son said to me, "Mom, I will never feel sorry for you."

I didn't think I liked the sound of that.

Then he explained, "You are such a together lady. You always have something cooking, something you're interested in. I can't see myself ever feeling sorry for you."

It was a compliment after all! I will gladly accept admiration in lieu of pity.

In order to fill those empty gaps in our lives, I believe it's important for us old ladies to set goals. According to the charts devised by those smart statisticians, I have fifteen to twenty years of living ahead of me. That's a long time, and maybe I won't make it for the full twenty, but I'm not going to worry about it. I might not live for another five years; who knows? I do know that the older I get, the faster time flies, and one thing I can do is formulate short-range plans. I can set goals for myself and take life in one-year chunks.

Think of the ways in which you would like your life to be different at the same time next year. Write these goals down. Then think of the things you will have to do in order to make these goals a reality. You have lived long enough to know that worthwhile things aren't handed to you on a silver platter. If we want something, we have to go for it.

You have the time, and this is important, so let's do it right. First, consider all the categories of your life: At the top of this list put Self. Are you mostly happy? Or sad, or lonely, or feeling nonproductive and useless? Are you active (doing what you enjoy doing), or do you mostly sit alone and watch TV? What is the quality of your life? Are you happy about it, or would you like to change?

Are you satisfied with your appearance? Do you need to take off some weight or put some on? What about your hair? Are you doing the most you can?

There are silver rinses and colors on the market that make the best of gray hair. What about your posture? Do you walk with your shoulders back, your chest out, and your tummy tucked in? (You should, you know.) Are you wearing glasses that are no longer stylish? Some of the new frames give your face an entirely different look. What about your clothes? Do they really suit you and the way you regard yourself? Take a long look at your skin, your nails, all the parts of you. Can your appearance be improved?

In other words, are you happy about yourself? If not, why not?

Next, consider your finances. List your income and assets on one side of a piece of paper and your liabilities (debts, etc.) on the other side. The difference is your net worth. This will probably be like a tonic. "Hey, I'm worth more than I thought I was!"

After studying your financial status, you may decide to save more money, or to spend more. Is there something you want or need? Devise a plan for getting it. We all have budgets—a certain amount for rent, for food, etc. But did you know that if you get in the habit of stashing away all the dollar bills (or five-dollar bills) in your wallet every time you return from shopping, in an amazingly short period of time you will have a nice little "bonus" to spend? I do this all the time.

Next on your list will be children. How are you getting along with them? In my case, I have to feel connected no matter where my children are. One lives on the West Coast, one here, the other there. In order to feel connected we have to communicate. One loves to write letters and send cards; another phones. One is able to drop in often. Think about how satisfying your connections are. Maybe with one or more you always get off on the wrong foot or one of you complains too much. What do you want these relationships to be like? What can you do to make them better? In many instances, it's quite simple. It is just a matter of seeing the problem and making up our minds to do something about it.

Other categories will be friends, grandchildren, neighbors, home, and so forth.

List each category; then write down the plusses and minuses for each. Think about how you want the relationship to be and what you can do to change the picture. You have your goals.

Perhaps you are just getting by, although comfortably enough, on your Social Security and a small pension. You would feel much more comfortable if you had more money in a savings account so that if you suffer an illness or have some other emergency, your independence won't go down the drain.

You can supplement your income. No, you don't have to go out looking for a job, but take a look at the things you can do. In the kitchen, in your sewing room, at your desk. Probably you can produce goods and/or services that people would be willing to pay for.

I have heard several young career women say that they would be more than willing to pay someone to hem their dresses.

Nearly every city has shopping malls, which are crowded with tables of homemade Christmas ornaments and decorations once a year. You pay a nominal fee to rent a table, and you sell the things you make.

Write poetry or short stories. They may never be published, but you can try. I know a woman in her nineties who mentioned casually to her pastor that she spent a lot of time writing poetry. The pastor asked to read some of it, published it in the church newsletter, sent the newsletter to a magazine, and the lady was published! It can happen!

Another talented old lady loves to draw. She is talking now with the author of children's books about illustrating some of them.

Another, who had always been a whiz at figures, went back to school and is now a CPA working on a free-lance basis.

Whatever it is you enjoy doing (which probably means you're good at it), do it. Go back to school if you have to in order to sharpen and update your skills. Work at it and become even better at what you do.

Many department stores and gift shops take homemade items on consignment. Look around, ask questions. Find a need and fill it. Maybe you can even create a need. Years ago, we didn't know that we needed a cake mix or sticks of ready-to-go piecrust. Someone created those items, and now we need them.

Some of us want to fill in the gaps in our lives with other things, and maybe we don't even know what those other things are. Take your time and think about it. What's the hurry? Perhaps choose one short-term goal: "Next week I am going to start walking every morning. I will start on Monday morning and walk for fifteen minutes." Then do it. It won't be long before you wouldn't skip that morning walk for anything in the world, and you will eventually be walking for more than fifteen minutes. You will have set a goal and accomplished it, and you will have filled in one of the gaps in your life.

I am not talking about keeping yourself busy every minute of the day. I know too many women who are on the go all the time, hopping into their cars and whizzing away here and there. If you're like them, you're already busy enough. Most of us enjoy our homes, our quiet times, but we don't want to drift with each day sort of sliding into the next. Goals are necessary to keep us on our toes. We need something to reach for in order to prevent becoming stale.

Some suggested short-term goals:

• I will take a trip (to visit someone, to see a new place, to go somewhere you have always wanted to see).

• I will make one new friend (an old lady neighbor, one of the children in the neighborhood, someone to whom you volunteer a service).

• I will get involved in one community/church activity (singing in the choir, delivering Meals-on-Wheels, joining a prayer chain).

• I will change my standard of living (move from your noisy family-type complex to an all-adult one; or vice versa).

The quickest way to grow into a miserable old lady is to stop having goals.

"My life is over. I have nothing to do."

"I can't do that. I'm too old."

Such a lot of baloney we feed ourselves!

When I was eligible for Social Security, I still worked at a job I had held for some while. One day I went to work, and by noon I had been laid off. Being laid off when you're young is bad enough. It means you have to hit the job-seeking trail again, and that's no fun.

Being laid off when you're old is a tragedy. I drove home that day in a fog. I was suddenly without a job after working nearly every day for over twenty years. I didn't even consider going out to try and find another job. That mountain was too high for me to climb.

A phone call saved my life. Was I free to travel around the country giving seminars for church secretaries? Was I free? You bet!

For over two years I ran through airports, drove rented cars down unfamiliar streets, and worked diligently. I had something to do!

Those days are in the past, and I am home all the time now. I have my writing, but that demands enormous self-discipline, which I'm not always up to.

You don't have to write books or give seminars or even be a whiz at sewing. Set a short-term goal for yourself. There must be things you want to accomplish, and you must expend some effort to get them. (If you don't want anything, and don't want to do anything, you have a problem, lady!)

Work the crossword puzzle in the newspaper every morning. It will keep your mind active. Pay attention to your appearance. For yourself. Every evening plan what you're going to do the next day. Defrost the refrigerator, clean the bathroom mirror, paste snapshots in the family album, write a letter. Plan something. You don't have to leave your home. Just don't let your days run into each other until they become a big blob of blank days.

Set aside a definite time each day to meditate. Let it be your quiet time that you look forward to. You may pray, or remember happy times, or plan something. Or simply empty your mind and let what will enter in. You will be surprised at what happens! Your subconscious will take over, your blood pressure will go down, and you will relax. God may speak to you.

Plans keep us going. We can have some short-range goals and some long-range goals and be working on them all the time.

If you don't reach your goals or your plans fail, don't retreat back into that realm of indifference and inactivity. Plan some alternatives.

My daughter and her family are planning to come here next Christmas. She has not spent a Christmas with me since she left home at age sixteen. I don't have to tell you the extent of my preparations. In May I pulled out all my favorite recipes and planned my menu for Christmas Day. I have already decided on the special decorations.

But what if something happens and I get a phone call in November: "Mother, we can't make it after all!"

How will I be able to cook and decorate and enjoy Christmas with my other children when my eyes are filled with tears and the lump in my throat won't go away?

I will enjoy Christmas because I have an alternate plan. For months I have been saving money for this significant holiday. If all goes as planned, I will have extra money to help make it special. If it doesn't go as planned, I am taking the other two members of my family somewhere else for Christmas. If we are lucky, it will be a cruise. If we're not so lucky, it will be overnight at a motel on the beach in Corpus Christi. It doesn't really matter which happens. Instead of sitting around, sadly wishing it could be different, we will celebrate Christmas in a different way.

Always have an alternate plan for the important things you want to do. I'm not talking about minor tasks like defrosting the refrigerator. If a friend calls and keeps you from getting that done, so what? It doesn't matter. But if you plan an important event that you look forward to for some time, form an alternate plan. Say to yourself, "If this doesn't work out, I will do something else."

We all have our "blob" days, of course. Every now and then I have a day or two when I do nothing. I lie on the couch and read, stare into space, or watch TV. I eat when and where and what I feel like eating. Some days I don't even get dressed. It feels good to stay in my nightgown and robe all day. Blob days are therapeutic and we should enjoy them; just don't allow them to become the rule rather than the exception.

Living day after day with the gaps in your life, refusing to accept challenges because you think you are too old, will make you old very quickly.

The longer you live in a rut, the harder it is to get out of it. You must stop worrying about yourself and get involved in a hobby or rewarding activity. Learn something new before your brain atrophies.

Remember: You are old—not out.

CHAPTER 12:

Grow in Your Faith

I guess the worst thing I could ever say to my teenagers was "Oh, grow up!" Whatever else they might be, the crowning insult was that they weren't grown up.

If someone told me to grow up, at my age, I would assume they meant that I am a foolish, naïve old woman.

We prefer to think that we are mature adults, and that we have learned many of the important lessons of life and know what it's all about.

Certainly in the matter of faith I am grown-up. I have attended Sunday church services nearly every Sunday of my life; I have attended and taught countless Bible study classes; I have said thousands of prayers, sung as many hymns.

Still, God has many truths to reveal to me. One time I studied a particular passage in the Bible, and it was just exactly what I needed at the moment. Years later, under entirely different circumstances, I read that same passage and received the comfort and direction I needed. Amazing!

I have heard people of the mature generation say, "Well, now I am old. I'm retired and don't have to work anymore. The children are all gone, living their own lives. I receive Social Security benefits, and I have a card that says I'm entitled to Medicare. Nobody needs me for anything, so I will just sit here and wait for death."

Oh, grow up!

I have heard older people lament about how long they have lived. "I have lived too many years. I have outlived my usefulness. I wish the Lord would take me."

Oh, grow up!

Some prattle on and on about the good old days when everything was better, finer, more decent. They prefer to live in the past and ignore the present. I remember the good old days, and they weren't so perfect. In fact, the good old days for me were during the Depression and World War II. They are certainly nothing to dwell on.

No matter how old we are, we are to continue growing in our faith. We need to pray more earnestly than ever for an increase in faith. Find some of the Bible passages that helped you so much when you were young, when you were a bride, when you were raising your children. They may hold new meanings for you now.

Just because you're old doesn't give you permission to sit in the rocking chair and figure that your time of giving and learning is past.

We are done with changing diapers and teaching little ones to pray. We have finished many races, but life is not over. Nobody needs you anymore? Great! It's about time! Count your blessings. Now you can concentrate on filling your mind and spirit with the gifts of God. You can listen to what He wants to tell you. You can concentrate on growing in your faith.

It's important for us to remember that God is always there and always has been, whether we have been aware of His presence or not. Surely there were many days when you were so busy with children and husband and balancing budgets and cooking that you simply didn't think about God. But He was thinking about you! At last you have the time and the quiet to concentrate on the fact that He is there waiting for you. Talk to God and listen. He has much to say to you.

CHAPTER 13:

How to Make the Most of Each Day

Sometimes Flash will say, "I didn't do one thing all day. I got up, I ate, I took a nap. That's about it. And it felt good."

I understand. Do-nothing days are a luxury we can finally enjoy. At first we feel a little guilty about them, but as time passes, the guilt vanishes and we just enjoy them. We have time to do more or less what we please.

A danger lurks here. The do-nothing days can become too frequent, and we can grow stale. Like it or not, regardless of age, we are responsible for how we spend the gift of time. I do not mean going out every day, joining organizations, volunteering to do dozens of tasks. I don't do those things, and neither does Flash. We both worked very hard for many years in church groups, and now we don't anymore. I am no longer much of a joiner. However, it is important to remember that we are stewards of our time. We may not do a lot, but we should pay attention to the quality of our actions.

You are healthy enough, even though you can't do all the things you once did, and your back gives out at the most inconvenient times, and you tire more quickly.

In the church, you have done your share of ar- ranging for potluck dinners, cleaning up in the kitchen, attending meetings, teaching in the Sunday school. You don't do that anymore. Leave it to the young women, you say; it's their turn.

You can handle just about anything that comes your way. After all, you have managed to endure the death of your husband, the loss of friends, the distance of your children, and the first years of loneliness. With God's help you're okay.

You have your memories, and you are smart enough to dwell on the happy ones and skim over the ones that hurt.

It has been a good life, with peaks of joy and hap- piness and a few valleys of pain. You have survived.

You rise early in the morning ready to face each new day. But what does each new day bring? Nothing. You eat your toast in silence while you read the morn- ing newspaper.

You put on your clothes, dust the furniture, pick up a few things here and there. You keep glancing at the clock. Time goes so slowly.

You make your bed, and as you straighten the spread, you think about your life. You planned it all so well. You and your husband did all the right things so that you would have this house to live in and enough money to live well and not worry about that. You have worked hard and raised your children, but now here you are. Alone. And not needed by anyone. You feel so useless you could cry.

You probably have quite a few years ahead of you, and they stretch out like a vast, empty desert. You never dreamed you would feel like this!

You know what you need, dear lady. Don't you?

In Ephesians 5:15–16 we read: "See then that ye walk circumspectly, not as fools, but as wise, redeeming the time, because the days are evil."

Redeeming the time is to number our days, to make the best of the time God has given us.

You may have used the years up to now as a good and faithful steward, but nowhere does Scripture say that you are excused from this once you are old.

Now, don't literally number your days in a dull monotone of counting them, marking them off on the calendar the way a prisoner does.

I was caught in that trap. Nobody needed me. Nobody cared very much whether I lived or died. My daughter liked to take long walks, but not with me. I walked too slowly. My bachelor son was proud of his cooking and prepared all the things I used to make for him.

When my son lived across town, he called me one day and said he was starving to death. (Oh, joyous words! He needed me!) It was several days until payday and he had no money, and could I help him out with a little food? (Oh, wondrous, magic words!) "I'll make your favorite casserole," I told him, "and my spaghetti sauce you like so much."

"Well, Mom, could you just send over the ingredients, please? I make those things a little differently than you do."

My casserole! Our family had eaten it for the last three generations. And my famous spaghetti sauce! I was too proud to ask him what he did that was different from what I did. With little grace, and no humor, I sent over the ingredients.

My son didn't yearn for my cooking. He only needed a few things to hold starvation at bay.

I not only counted the days, I counted the hours. "It's only ten o'clock. My soap opera doesn't come on for three hours. What am I going to do until then?"

Often I would look ahead and be dismayed by the thought that I could have fifteen or twenty years of life yet. I didn't want to live that long. I didn't have anything to do!

Go ahead, bet your life. Take a stance. Choose something to do. Accept a challenge. It will probably take some nerve to get dressed and go out and volunteer to do something, but believe me, there are people who need you. Scan the newspaper. Nearly every day you will find "Volunteers needed."

Take a long walk every morning. Commune with

nature, greet fellow walkers, and smile. It's a grand beginning for a day.

Work with the young women in the church or in some community facility. I believe that we older women have a grave responsibility to young women. If we huddle in our dark corners, leading lonely lives, counting the inactive days, we are inadvertently telling young women: "This is all you have to look forward to." And that's a lie! Good days lie ahead, and we should live them up to the hilt. Recognize your stewardship of time.

If your church or neighborhood doesn't have a group for the Ripened Generation, start one. Let a whole bunch of you show the younger people that life is worth living and can be a joyful, interesting experience, no matter how long it lasts.

When I was a young woman I knew an extraordinary elderly lady. She was a hard-nosed retired nurse who accepted no nonsense from anyone. Although her face was rather stern and deeply lined, her blue eyes glistened with vitality. Each new day, each new acquaintance was a challenge to her, and she taught me several useful things.

She helped me understand the healing properties of hope. "A positive attitude will do more than an aspirin," she told me every time I complained of an ache or a pain. The years proved her right. I haven't taken a pain killer in many years. One time I was crying about a wart on my hand. She told me to go out and find some milkweed and put the milk on the wart and it would disappear. To this day I know nothing about the wart-vanishing properties of milkweed but I do know that I searched diligently for milkweed, believing with all my heart that it would make the hated wart disappear, and I found some and applied the milk and the wart vanished. Was it the milkweed or was it my belief that it would work that did the trick? This woman occupied a very brief period of my life, and has been dead for many years, but she gave me a glimpse of what a beautiful old lady can be. She never stopped being interested in whatever life offered, and never did she sit back and say, "I'm too old to participate." She was actively involved in life to the very end. I will always be grateful to her for giving me that positive picture of old age. I want to do the same for the young women I know. Don't you?

How to Get Along with Family and Friends

CHAPTER 14:

Treasure Your Independence

Independence is a funny thing. You can fight for it, insist on it, demand it. And you can grow soft around the edges and find yourself enjoying having other people wait on you and cater to you because you're an old lady.

This is a velvet-lined trap, and you don't even know it's a trap because it is so comfortable. I urge you to be aware of it and don't allow yourself to fall into it. You are perfectly capable of taking care of yourself. You can clean your house and do your laundry and rake the leaves in your yard. You know you can do these things (and much more) and you also know that you should do these things. However, if there is a loving person or two around who insists on doing these tasks for you because you're old, they're lining the trap. Don't let them. It's patronizing, even though their intentions are good, and you have to stand up and say, "I'll do it myself, thank you." It is too easy to sit back and tell yourself that you're letting them wait on you because it makes them feel good. Let them feel good about doing something else, not robbing you of your independence. Settling into this trap isn't fair to you or to the ones who are lining the trap.

My daughter Heide is a lovely, generous, and loving young woman. The older I get, the more she does for me. Her husband even loves me. (Thank you, Lord!)

I love Heide so much and appreciate her attentiveness. Every time she stops in to see me, she takes my trash out and asks if there is anything I need. Going to the library, she carries my heavy book bag. I protest. She responds, "No mother of mine carries things while I'm around."

Once in a while I feel as though I am walking a precarious tightrope. On one hand, I want to assert my independence and tell Heide that I am perfectly capable of doing just about everything for myself. (I am!)

On the other hand, I don't want to push this considerate daughter away. However, one day I felt myself slowly sinking into that velvet-lined trap, and I caught myself just in time.

My other daughter had sent me a pair of clown masks. Heide said, "The next time I come over, I'll hang them on the wall of your study."

I said, "Okay."

A couple of days passed. The masks lay on the couch. Then I saw what was happening. I said to myself, "What in the world is wrong with you, old lady? You can't hang two masks on a wall?" My reliance on Heide made me very angry with myself.

So I dragged out the small step stool, got the hammer and nails, and hung the masks on the wall.

When Heide came over she said, "Oh, I see you hung your masks. They look great."

Do you see the danger I was in? It is very easy to lose your independence, and it's one of the worst things that can happen to you.

Sometimes my kids laugh at my little spurts of independence, but I don't believe they would have me be any other way. In the long run, it wears well for all of us.

My dear Pastor Larson offered one day to arrange for people to transport me to and from church on Sunday mornings.

I told him no thanks. I would take a taxi or whatever I had to do to get to church, but I would do it on my own.

Pastor said, "Oh, Jane, you're so independent!"

I agreed.

Then he said, "But I guess that's one of the things I like about you."

So hang on to your independence, dear ladies. Keep a firm grip. That velvet-lined trap is smothering.

How often have you heard: "What a shame! One woman cared for ten children, and now those ten children can't care for that one woman."

Unless you're ill or crippled, that statement makes no sense at all.

Why should those ten children care for you? You raised them from birth, and watched them leave the nest one by one.

You brought those children into the world and loved and nurtured and trained them. Of course you did. It's what you wanted to do. It was your fulfilling happiness for years.

Take pride in them, relive the wonderful days, spend hours poring over baby books. But don't spoil it by muttering, "Look what I did for you. Now you owe me."

The truth, dear lady, is that they don't owe you anything. They don't owe you money or love or respect. You are old enough to know that these things are earned.

Take care of yourself the best you possibly can. If you have earned your children's love and respect, you will get all the attention you want from them.

Once in a while, if you truly need something from them, you will find them willing and eager to respond.

If you haven't earned their love and respect, your whining and nagging will only drive them away.

We old ladies generally tend to concentrate on ourselves. When we were young, certain aches and pains intruded, but we were too busy to pay much attention to them. We popped an aspirin or two and kept on with what we were doing. We had to.

Now, a headache or a backache looms in our lonely lives. We almost find ourselves welcoming these minor pains because they break the boredom; they give us something to talk about.

So when one of our children calls, our opening words are, "I have a terrible headache. I hope there is nothing seriously wrong. It throbs and throbs. I could hardly sleep last night."

Oh, lady, give me a break! You know it wasn't that bad and you are using a very slight discomfort as a bid for attention and sympathy.

Your child may be, and probably is, struggling with many problems: keeping a marriage going, paying the bills, raising children, all the things you once struggled with.

If your conversations focus on a headache blown out of proportion, or how lonely you are, or accusations of "You never call" or "Why didn't you write?" is it any wonder they stay away from you?

By laying a guilt trip on them, you're only adding to their burdens. And you are not hanging on to your independence.

I know it's difficult not to criticize or grumble. When your children don't write to you, or call you on any kind of a regular basis, you feel neglected and unloved. Well, you are neglected, but probably not unloved. You do feel that they owe you at least a letter now and then. You're their mother and you love them, and the least they could do is let you know how they're doing. It's a very difficult thing to come to terms with, but you must. Your children don't owe you a single thing. If they love you, and if they are thoughtful, considerate people, they will write or call. Most young people aren't that thoughtful or considerate. They are fine people and you're proud of them, but they simply don't think of you sitting by the phone, or watching for the mail carrier just to hear from them. Accept that fact with good grace. If you are guarding and cherishing your independence, it will be easier.

Another thing: They are watching you grow old. They see all the changes. In a way, you force them to prelive their own old age. They know it is going to happen to them eventually.

Ask young people, as I did, if they ever think about growing old. Always, the answer is no. "Well, sure, I know I'll be old someday. But I never think about it."

They don't want to think about it. And if you keep forcing them to think about the various negative aspects of aging, they will resent you. They are not going to want to spend much time with you. And who can blame them?

What a nice gift you can give them by demonstrating how wonderful old age can be. Forget about your headache or joint ache and the imagined slights and adopt a positive attitude. Let your children know about the great compensations of old age.

When your daughter tells you about her problems

with the children, sympathize with her, offer advice only if it is requested, and then tell her that one day her job will be finished and then she can enjoy the benefits of old age like you are.

Cherish your independence, your freedom from so many restrictions, and stop complaining. Show the young people that you are having a marvelous time and that they have something to look forward to.

CHAPTER 15:

Keep Friends in Your Life

Sometimes, as a joke, I will look at my children for a long time. Long enough so that they will say, "Mom, why are you staring at me?" And I will shrug and smile and say, "Oh, never mind. I love you anyway."

It's a joke, but it's oh, so true. In spite of anything they do, any hurt they inflict on me, any careless word they throw my way, any failure in their lives, I love them anyway.

When you have lived for many years, you can appreciate how rare a love like that is. God loves me that way. He knows my failures and faults, and He loves me anyway.

My children love me anyway, too. I am far from perfect and do things that annoy them, and I can be stubborn as a mule . . . but they love me anyway.

It might not be a bad idea for preachers to ask the bride and groom: "Do you promise to love and cherish each other anyway?"

We need friends who love us anyway. We need them especially now that we're getting old. It's crucial that we don't rely on family to fill all of our emotional needs.

How often have you heard: "I lived my life for my children. Now they don't need me for anything!"

How often have you said that? I've got to tell you: You will receive your reward in heaven, okay? For now, it would be a wise thing to hold on to your friends and to cultivate some new friendships.

Over a lifetime we make many acquaintances. However, most of us can count our dear friends on one hand and have fingers and a thumb left over. Friends who know you and love you anyway. One dear, true friend in a lifetime is rare.

We need friends. I have one friend who knows everything about me: my failings, the tragedies I have borne, and my weaknesses. She was by my side at the times I was my most unlovely self. She loves me anyway.

The only way to have a friend is to be a friend. Maybe that's why so many old ladies are so lonely: they want friends, but they haven't tried to be a friend. Some are like soggy old sponges: they take in but they don't give out.

Poor Mary isn't a very comfortable person to be with. I know that she doesn't care about me. She is too busy making sure I know how lonely she is, how miserable she feels, how much she wishes life were different. She is too needy! I have talked to many old ladies who are obsessed with how terrible life is now that they're old. They gripe about their failing health, their insomnia, their children's inconsiderate behavior. They talk on and on, listing their grievances, until I want to scream at them.

My friend Flash, on the other hand, is not a needy person, and she frees me to love her and enjoy her company. She is interesting because she reads, and she likes to discuss subjects besides her health and the things old age is doing to her.

Flash said once, "No one can make me angry. No one!" I thought about that a lot. Our youthful years were filled with anger. Parents infuriated us because they didn't let us do the things we wanted to do.

We blew hot and cold on friendships, loves, jobs. I have watched my children stamp their feet and rave and rant and vent their anger at teachers, bosses, friends, and at me.

Sometimes it looks so silly! I have experienced those situations, and I know what they're feeling. I mutter to myself, "Thank goodness I'm past that stage."

I like Flash's philosophy better. It is a good sign of a great old lady to state with conviction: "Absolutely no one can make me angry."

If you like people, people are going to like you.

Poor Mary looks down her nose at everyone who doesn't dress as she does, think as she does, worship the way she does.

It's easy to dismiss people based on how they look or act. Because of the number of years we have lived, we think we know it all. But we don't realize how much we're missing. After I grew older, I had to train myself to be interested in people. When I was young, curiosity seemed to come naturally, but as I grew older, it diminished. I don't know why, but I guess we become a bit jaded. When you have done anything over and over for so many years, you don't feel much like doing it anymore. I was beginning to feel that way about people. I had my family and a few good friends, and I assumed I didn't need anyone else. That kind of an attitude leads to a very lonely old age.

I discovered the hard way that we have to train ourselves to be open to others. My children, who for so long had been everything to me, left. They left one by one in alarming haste, and then I was alone. They were out there living their lives, and that simply was the end of that. A very big part of my life was gone. Some of my friends moved away, a few of them died. I moved to an apartment and felt like a stranger to the world. The people within my special circle of love were no longer there. I felt like holing up in my apartment, closing the drapes, and wallowing in my lonely misery. In fact, I did exactly that for a while. Thank goodness, a few people I met showed me a different way.

The people you meet in this new life won't be perfect. This one will talk on and on about her children and grandchildren until you feel like hitting her; that one can talk about nothing but soap operas. Don't shut them out. Listen to them, talk to them, practice patience with them. They are the same ladies who will bring you a bowl of hot soup when you're not feeling well, and will be company when you're lonely enough to climb the walls. They are the ones who will stroll with you in the evenings, comfort you when you need uplifting, and rejoice with you in your triumphs. That's what friendship is all about.

Once in the airport in Dallas, I had time to kill between flights. I roamed around until I came to the magazine and book stand. An old lady was there, killing time, too, leafing through magazines.

She was gray-haired and tiny and she wore tight jeans, a blue denim vest over a white shirt, elaborate white boots, and a hat you wouldn't believe. I guess you could call it a cowgirl hat—a Stetson—with a quivering bouquet of feathers on one side.

Ordinarily, I would have passed her by with a chuckle. Silly old lady! But I was in training to like people, so I went up to her and said, "I love the way you look."

"Why, thanks, sugar!" she replied. "I like it, too."

That lovely Texas lady and I wound up having lunch together, and she told me why she was dressed as she was. No, she wasn't a rancher's or a cowboy's wife. She simply liked the look. She got a huge kick out of knowing that people did a double take when she walked by. "Some think I'm crazy, I know," she said, "but that's better than not being noticed at all."

She told me that she was seventy years old and that she wasn't waiting to catch a flight to anywhere.

Whenever she was in the mood, she dressed up and roamed around the airport for a few hours, letting people watch her.

Isn't that marvelous? See what I would have missed if I had stared at her, dismissed her as simply an odd sort of person, and gone on my superior way?

I will never forget that particular old lady. Who knows, if I am ever lucky enough to see her again, she may be dressed like an Indian squaw, or . . .

I know an old lady who moaned and groaned for a while because she claimed that God had not blessed her with any gifts. She was not artistic, she couldn't speak in public, she was a lousy seamstress, and she hated to cook. It seemed to her that everyone she knew had been blessed with some special gift and she had been behind the door when they were passed around.

Then one day a wise person told her that she did have a gift. She was a servant.

That did not please this lady at all. She most certainly didn't think of herself as a servant. In fact, when her husband was alive, they had a big home and entertained regularly. She hired and fired servants.

"You are the type of person," this sage friend told her, "who likes to help people, to make them comfortable. If we lived in ancient times with dusty roads, you would be the one to remove your guests' sandals and wash their feet."

It was true. She really listened to people and cared about them. Anyone could talk on and on to this lady and never get the feeling that her own words were on the tip of her tongue waiting for the talker to stop and take a breath of air.

What a marvelous gift she had! She cared about people and wanted them to be comfortable in her presence. She had been blessed with the gift of servanthood.

Another old lady wanted to be interesting. She wanted people to desire her companionship. So she became interested. Her son was studying physics and loved to talk about it. She got some books and studied as hard as she could just so she could at least listen intelligently.

I asked her once if she understood what she read. (I can't even begin to make sense out of the dictionary definition of physics!)

Her answer was no, she didn't understand it at all,

but after a few hours of study, she was able to ask a few fairly intelligent questions.

Her son loves to talk to her, and he tells his friends, "My Mom is really into physics."

If you want to be an interesting old lady, be interested. Learn things so that you have something to talk about besides yourself.

You don't have to have a fat savings account to be an interested, interesting old lady. The public library is free. Or you can do what a friend of mine does. Once a week she goes to a large shopping mall, sits on a bench, and does some people watching. She almost always gets into a conversation with someone, and she always comes home feeling like she has been to a party. Her children call her at the end of her people-watching days. They don't make the call as a duty, but because they are anxious to hear about her day at the mall. She always has something interesting and/or funny to relate.

If you can't get out to the airport or the library or the mall, do something interesting at home. Oh, yes, you can! You can call people and tell them you were thinking about them and just wanted to hear their voice. Once they get over the shock, they will love you for it.

Write letters. Letter writing is a fast-disappearing art, and you can help keep it alive. Practice writing beautiful letters. You could even get an inexpensive kit and learn how to do calligraphy.

You can step outside your door now and then and talk to your neighbors.

My ninety-three-year-old mother-in-law always carries a plate of home-baked cookies to anyone moving into her neighborhood. I suspect hers is the only welcoming visit the newcomers receive.

The energy of love and caring has to flow in both directions or it will die. Many times I have just settled down for an afternoon nap, or a TV movie, or a quiet cup of coffee, and someone knocks on the door. It is someone wanting to visit. If I want friends, and if I want these dear ladies to keep coming to see me, I must welcome them. A missed nap or TV show or cup of coffee must never take precedence over a person. I like the love and attention flowing toward me, but it must be a two-way street.

It is indeed true that the more love you give, the more you get. There simply is no excuse for being a lonely old lady.

You can be fun to know. Certainly, I don't have the sort of fun I had in my youth anymore, and I even find it difficult to define fun. What some people call fun sounds dull or immoral to me. I don't want to party or try to find someone to dance with me. Fun has a different meaning now. But we can have fun. In fact, we should try to have some fun every day.

My son loves Garfield the cat. So every morning I cut that comic strip out of the paper, and once a week I mail him the collection, along with a cheerful note. That's fun.

When I read or hear a funny joke, I write it down. (I can't ever remember the punch line!) I save it for the times when I am with certain people and I want to share a laugh. That's fun.

I dry all kinds of vegetables and fruits: potatoes, lemons, limes, artichokes, etc. I let them dry out in the air until they shrivel and change shape and color. I have a plate full of these and get a kick out of asking people if they can guess what they are. Sometimes they can; other times they are amazed when I tell them. It's a moment of fun.

Sometimes calling a friend and sharing the details of some idiotic thing you did is fun. "You will never believe what I did today!" you say, and then you laugh about it together. That's fun.

However you do it, or whatever is fun for you, look for it as often as you can. Unless you do, you can go for a very long time without laughing once. Doesn't that sound terrible? Doesn't that sound like a bitter, lemony old lady?

It's a good idea for us old ladies to plan our days, at least part of the time. Because if we don't, those days march on relentlessly, and the next thing we know, we have spent a month—or a year—doing nothing.

You know what happens to an arm or a leg if it isn't used. It atrophies. It withers up and becomes useless. If you don't use yourself, stir up your old bones, that is what will happen to you. Once or twice a week at least, plan the next day.

Tomorrow I will walk for an hour; I will call Elsie and ask how she's doing; I will go to the cafeteria for lunch; I will test that new recipe I've been wanting to try.

Plan something. I overheard a young person talking about her mother. "Oh, she's home. She is always home; you can be sure of that!"

Do you know what I would like people to say about me? "You never know where she is or what she's up to."

We must build our people resources. We have peaks and valleys in our life, highs and lows, and it is a terrible thing not to have anyone to share them.

You receive a phone call telling you that you have a brand-new grandchild. You have to share that with someone! You need to have someone congratulate you and tell you how happy they are for you. Good news has to be shared.

Crying all alone is a very sad thing! We have to sink into the valleys at times, and we need our friends to go with us. We need to have them give us a loving hug, to cry with us, to let us know they understand.

If you are there with a smile and congratulations

when others have a stroke of good luck, and if you are there with a hug and understanding when they suffer, they will be there for you when you need them. None of these good things will happen, however, unless we first reach out to make friends.

CHAPTER 16

Stop Playing Games with Your Children

When your children were quite young, you were an all-important figure in their lives. Even though you weren't completely aware of it all the time, and probably didn't give it much thought one way or the other, you had great power over them.

First, they feared that you might leave them; if you walked out of their lives, what would happen to them? I recall a day when my six-year-old son and I were shopping in a large department store and somehow got separated. In only a few minutes I responded to a voice on an intercom saying that a little blond boy was lost.

He was in an absolute state of panic, as frightened as he had ever been in his life. To tell the truth, so was I. We spent a few shaky moments comforting each other with hugs and kisses.

Second, they always feared that you would stop loving them. You never, ever threatened that, or even thought it, but the apprehension was in their minds nevertheless.

Have I been so bad that Mama won't love me anymore?

Third, if you had more than one child, there was sibling rivalry to contend with. Does Mama love Susie more than she loves me? You were aware of these feelings and did nothing to foster them, but they remained nevertheless. Sibling rivalry seems to come with the package.

Fourth, they feared punishment. If Mom finds out I did that, will she spank me, or not let me have dessert, or will she send me to bed early?

Now we are through with all those childish things. Or are we?

Do you still try to wield power over your children even though they are married, living apart from you? Think about it. I know many older women who wield this power in one or all of the ways they did when their children were young. In those days, you didn't want them to feel that you would ever stop loving them or that you would desert them. You did everything you could to dispel those fears. "Mommy loves you. I will always love you. You are my dear child. I will always be here."

You tried very hard to remove sibling rivalry. If you did something special for one of the children, you made sure the others weren't slighted. You deplored this rivalry. All mothers have built-in scales in their heads to weigh the favors and gifts so that rivalry is reduced and things come out as evenly as possible.

Of course, you had to discipline them. That was part of your job as a parent, to teach them that when they chose to disobey the rules, they had to suffer the consequences.

You may not be completely aware of it—and again, you may know exactly what you're doing—but in either case, if you are still manipulating your children, the only message for you is: Stop it!

I have seen lonely old women play the game of "I won't love you anymore" with their grown children. They never say that in so many words, but the implication is there.

"You never call or write. I thank God your brother isn't like that."

"Thank you for the birthday card, even if it was late. I got the most beautiful flowers from your sister."

"Jenny stopped in this morning. Your sister is so thoughtful."

In other words, if you don't love me, I will just have to accept that and lavish my love on someone else. It's sad, and it hurts, but I guess that's the thanks I get.

How many of her children does it take to replace a light bulb for this kind of old woman?

Why, none. She says, "Never mind. You don't care about me anymore, and I don't care either. You don't have to do anything for me. Someone will come along who will care enough. In the meantime, I'll just sit here in the dark."

Some women see a great opportunity to use sibling rivalry as a way of getting attention.

"Your sister is so good to me," Mom says to her son. "She never fails to call and ask how I'm doing or if I need anything."

Not to be outdone by that foot-kissing sister, Sonny offers to stop by every Friday night after work for a visit.

The next day Mom makes a phone call. "Your brother is so good to me. Guess what he is going to do every Friday?"

And on goes Manipulating Mama, and it works for a while.

The trouble with this little game is that her children are going to wind up hating each other to some degree, and that's not what any mother wants.

Also, they just may see through Mom's little strategy and refuse to play.

Punishment was and still is a powerful weapon. It can come in many forms now.

"I'm thinking of rewriting my will."

"Don't bother about me. I asked my neighbor to take me to the doctor. She was glad to do it."

"You go on to the restaurant. I didn't think you would invite me, so I just had a sandwich."

If you are guilty of playing any of these games with your children, shame on you. What you need to do is to build a life for yourself that would at least be a satisfactory one if all your children moved to a remote island with no telephones.

You must. A hobby, a special interest, interaction with friends, or volunteer work can fill enough of your life and keep you interested and interesting.

You might be in for a big surprise: Once the games stop, your offspring may come to you.

CHAPTER 17:

Don't Be an Old Lady Manipulator

Naturally, you would say that you never have and never will manipulate your children (or even close, longtime friends). However, manipulation is a great temptation. In our loneliness, we're sure our children and friends have forgotten about us. We pout that they don't really care how or if we're getting along, if our health is okay, if we're happy.

We don't actually plan the manipulation. It comes naturally. And we have lived long enough to know exactly how to play the game and usually win.

When one person calls or visits, we are always upbeat. We're doing just fine, and feeling great. Why, life couldn't be better.

The truth is, we have discovered that it is almost impossible to win any sympathy from this particular person. He or she has no patience with complaining or depressed people. So if we want this person to keep calling, coming around, liking us, we have to put on a happy face and assure him or her that we're on top of the world.

However, we give another person (usually a brother or sister to the other one) an entirely different reaction to the question "How are you doing?" Every time this person calls or visits, we are in terrible shape. We are worried sick about a pain in our hip, or we nearly coughed to death last night. Our appetite is so poor; we wonder aloud what that means.

You know that this person will immediately respond with attention and sympathy. "Shall I take you to the doctor?" (Of course not!) "I'll make a special casserole for you." (That would be nice.) "I'll run out now and get some cough medicine. I worry about you, living here alone." (And I am going to keep you worrying.)

What a fraud you are! You're liable to be found out, you know. One of these days those two people may get together and start comparing notes, and then the game will be over.

A much happier and healthier way for you to get attention from both of them and ease your loneliness at the same time is to develop an interest in something. Start a hobby or join an exercise class for women our age. Try bird-watching. Go to the library and check out a book on birds. They are fascinating creatures, and simply watching them and identifying them can give hours of pleasure. Nearly every community has a bird-watching group you can join.

Collecting things is a passive recreation that you can do as a sideline. Don't collect salt and pepper shakers, though. Choose something a little unusual, even outrageous, like Mexican crosses or cloisonné. You know about my clown collection. Nobody ever knows what to buy old ladies for birthdays or Christmas. "They don't need or want anything!" is a familiar cry. The old ladies say, "There is nothing I need or want." However, think of the lift you will give the gift buyers if you have a hobby of collecting rather unusual objects. Give your mind something to think about besides yourself.

One old lady, awash in her loneliness for a long time, was constantly muttering, "I just don't understand my children." One night she saw a TV special on illiteracy. An avid reader, she considered the inability to read one of life's worst deprivations. She could imagine old ladies, lonesome like herself, feeling abandoned and not having the solace of books to read.

The next day she called the number on the TV screen and offered her services. "I am not a teacher," she told them. "Can you read?" she was asked. "Oh, yes, I can do that." The man answered, "Then we need you."

She is now embarked on a satisfying project which

has dispelled much of her loneliness and given her something besides herself to think about. If you want to do this, call your public library for information. You could even read for a children's story hour.

Do something. Create unique bookmarks, collect baskets to hang on a wall, write poetry. Attend department store fashion shows or local concerts, dry some flowers, or collect rocks. The important thing is to detract from your preoccupation with yourself, your loneliness, your health, and how your children are ignoring you, so that you won't have to play games to attract their attention.

Now, I am not advocating that you do any of these things to please anyone but yourself. You could say, "All right, already! I'll collect rocks!" If you decide to collect rocks, do it with a definite purpose in mind. If you are selective as to the shape and texture and color of stones and rocks, you can glue certain ones together and make birds and people and animals. It might take a dab of paint for eyes and a mouth or beak. This can be a most interesting and entertaining hobby.

Another thing some old ladies do is insist that they are fine when they're not. Oh, deliver me from them! They stick out their brave little chins and say, "Why, I'm doing just great." Although everyone knows they're not, they simply can't bear to break that wonderful display of "spirit."

126

The children have to go to the store for her or she doesn't eat. She not only hates taking a taxi to the store, but is a little afraid of leaving her home, so she does without. Her children have learned not to ask her if she's eating well. They know she will say she is. They check her cupboard and refrigerator and then do her shopping for her. They remember well the time she fainted and bravely admitted that she hadn't eaten for two days.

She always says, with that courageous little smile, "There isn't a thing in the world I need." Her children regularly check her supply of underwear and hosiery.

The problem is, this woman is not the brave little soul she tries to make people think she is. She knows what's going on, how she is being cared for, and she continues to play the game.

It could be that she is afraid of admitting a weakness of any kind, because if she did, her children might decide that it would be best to put her into a nursing or retirement home. So she puts up a valiant front whereby she is telling her children: "See how well I'm doing. Don't even think of a home for me."

She is being very selfish. Her children are running themselves ragged playing the charade with her.

Wouldn't it be better for this woman to admit how she feels about taxis and going shopping alone? She could simply ask her children, "Could you fit me in on your shopping days?" Admit whatever problems you have, and together work out a solution that will be the easiest for everyone.

You are the one with all the unscheduled time, so try to fit into their schedule and be grateful if they're willing to help. The truth is, you will last a lot longer on your own if you do that, instead of playing the brave little old lady game.

Then there are the old ladies who suffer mysterious dizzy spells or whose hearts beat too fast (or too slow). These spells come on at the most convenient times (for the old ladies, that is) and are always accompanied by a vague wave of the hand and the insistence "Oh, don't pay any attention. I'm all right, really I am. Just give me a minute to pull myself together."

Why, shame on you! I will admit I did this very thing for a while. I scared my kids half to death, but when I refused to see a doctor and my spells occurred only in their presence, my kids figured it out. The only thing is, I am pretty much in the same position as the little boy who cried wolf once too often.

One day both of my grown children were in my living room watching TV. I went into the kitchen, put some meat under the broiler, and it caught fire. I yelled. My kids paid no attention. As I turned off the broiler and beat at the flames, I could hear them laughing at something on the TV. I finally had to scream, "This is real! I've got a fire in here!" to convince them to come and help me.

Don't play games. If you suspect something is wrong with you, go to a doctor and find out.

When my daughter was little, she tried tricks to get attention. One of them was telling me that she didn't feel well. I recognized her tactic, so I would take her temperature and then say, "You have a case of spring fever, but thank goodness I know how to cure it."

I put her to bed in a darkened room with a glass of Kool-Aid nearby and instructed her to rest. It never took more than twenty minutes for her to emerge from her room smiling. "I'm cured of spring fever. May I go out and play?"

If you keep moaning and groaning for sympathy, eventually your kids will do the same thing to you. They will relegate you to your room until you figure out for yourself that you are miraculously cured. Unless, that is, you raised an exceptionally stupid brood, and I doubt that very much.

Another trick old ladies try to pull is putting themselves down. Probably we're all guilty of this, but we should stop it.

The kids ask us to go to a movie with them. We reply, "Oh, no, thank you. Who wants an old lady along? I would just cramp your style."

Or: We are all looking at family snapshots, and you hold up one picture. "Look how pretty I used to be. Oh, it's terrible growing old."

Or: "I'm sorry I can't keep up with you young folks. These old legs aren't much use anymore."

You know why we do this, don't you? It's called fishing for compliments. We wait to hear the expected responses:

"You're not old. We'd love to have you with us."

"You're still pretty. Of course you are."

"You're doing fine. Why, you're just a spring chicken."

Oh boy, we are really hard up for compliments, aren't we?

What we're doing is making the negative picture of old ladies even more negative. In other words, we are perpetuating a lie. Old age isn't ugly or disabling. Not usually. We have to make up our minds that we are going to show young people the many good things about old age. Talk about how wonderful it is not to have to set the alarm to go to a job, or to take care of a household. You don't have to fight rush-hour traffic. Such freedom! You can sleep in late if you feel like it, or you can get up before the sun and roam around in a peaceful silence.

You can take a nap in the afternoon. You can eat your meals on a tray before the TV. Play up all the positive aspects of old age. Some of us may have to search for them, but that's valuable, too. Let the young people in your life know that many bonuses await them when they grow old.

Another trick some old ladies try to pull is the money scam. You don't need a fortune to play this game, although if you're wealthy, or reasonably so, you can play it on a grander scale than most of us. All you need is a certain amount of discretionary income.

You can keep everyone in your family in line, doing exactly what you want them to do. Just keep sweetly reminding them that you hold the purse strings, and if you are going to let loose of any of your money, you expect certain considerations from them. This ploy is extremely tacky, but I have seen it work.

You can get them to pay attention to you, take you places, do things for you, treat you nicely. In return, you buy things for them, help them pay for luxuries they can't afford, and if they take you out to eat, it's your treat.

This sort of bribery is tacky, and I hope that none of you indulge in it. We don't want love and attention from our family that we have to pay for.

We old ladies do play some of these games, and we usually win. After all, we have had years of experience and we know the rules. However, beware! Sometimes the children wise up, or one maverick in the family refuses to play, and then they get together and talk about what you have been doing. If you are very lucky, they will laugh it off and let you know that they won't fall for your tricks anymore. They could resent you, decide they can't trust you, and leave you alone. Also, they will have a distorted picture of what being old is really like. You might get away with your tricks for a while, perhaps even for a long while, but not forever.

Eventually, you're going to be found out, and then you will know that it wasn't worth it.

CHAPTER 18:

Living with
Your Children

Way back in the old days, when Mother became old around fifty or fifty-five, she made her home with one of her children. That's just the way it was, and everyone accepted it as graciously as they could.

That is not the custom today, at least in this country. Mother isn't considered old until she hits sixty-five. And she is an active, independent lady. The last thing she wants to do is to move in with one of her children.

She doesn't want to live in a nursing home or a retirement home, either. If she is a widow, in spite of many lonely hours, she prefers living by herself.

We old ladies of today are fiercely independent, sometimes even foolishly so, but independence is one of the things we don't want to lose, and we cling to it. I have known a few women who were forced to live with their children following an illness, but they kept their apartments, continuing to pay the rent, because they would "be returning home any day now."

Young people have some hang-ups concerning this. They feel obligated to ask Mother to make their home with them. It's what they are supposed to do, and if they don't extend the invitation, they feel guilty.

Old ladies say: "I will never live with one of my children."

And: "There is no way you will get me into a nursing or retirement home."

Sons and daughters say: "I couldn't stand having her live with us. She would never in a million years understand our life-style, but we have to ask her."

And: "My wife (or husband) simply wouldn't put up with having her live with us."

And: "It will be rough, but I don't feel that I have a choice. She's my mother."

Sometimes children, out of a sense of duty, or to escape those nagging guilt feelings, will insist that Mother live with them. And Mother, secretly afraid of living on her own, just getting a taste of loneliness, gives in. The arrangement doesn't work for any number of predictable reasons, and both sides suffer hurt feelings. The children feel more guilty than ever, and mother has lost valuable time that should have been spent learning how to live alone.

We old ladies of today can take care of ourselves, and we want our children to accept that fact and let us do it. We know how to ride a bus or call a taxi. We know how to order from catalogs and call for a pizza to be delivered. We make friends, we write letters, and we talk on the phone. We learn how to handle the lonely times and the losses. We want to be left alone to discover what we have gained and how we can use these gains to our best advantage.

The happiest decision I made was to get out of a house and into an apartment. I loved the house, but there were several duties connected with it I didn't love very much as I grew older. The grass had to be mowed on a regular basis, faucets dripped, and things went wrong that required a service person. Most of my neighbors were young couples with small children. I couldn't walk around the neighborhood because dogs barked at me and nipped at my heels.

Then I moved to an apartment. I was still surrounded by my familiar furniture and lamps and pictures, so I felt at home as soon as I was settled in. Someone else mows the lawn and tends to the flowers. If a faucet drips or a light switch doesn't work, I call the office and someone comes to fix it.

My apartment complex is an adult community, no children allowed. If we want to, we tenants meet several times a day in a lovely courtyard. We watch out for each other. When one is ill, casseroles are cooked and help is offered. If one doesn't open the living room drapes by afternoon, someone checks to be sure all is well.

Three laps around the complex is exactly one mile. The only dogs running around are on a leash. I get out every morning and walk past the beautiful Gulf of Mexico, past a lovely, peaceful cemetery and a parking lot. Every morning I meet several other walkers, and we greet each other like family.

With the locks on my doors and windows, the well-lighted courtyards, and the presence of a security guard, I feel safe and secure.

We have two swimming pools—and if you would like to smile, watch the daily procession of old ladies in bathing suits, carrying their inner tubes, marching to the pool. I dearly love them.

The apartment managers love us old ladies. We pay our rent on time, don't damage the property, take care of one another, do not play loud music or give wild parties, and some of us even beautify the area. Many have hanging plants and boxes of flowers and bird feeders in the trees. On my walks, I have seen tomatoes and cabbage growing in a border of plants.

Other housing possibilities are surfacing every day. Some old people live in an apartment complex with a large community room. They watch TV together, play cards, socialize. In some, they cook the evening meal together. More and better alternatives are sure to come to light as our population of over sixty grows.

Loneliness doesn't seem so terrible if you consider the alternative: living with one of your children. Imagine having to be constantly on the alert so that you mind your own business, that you don't interfere with their routine, even struggling probably to maintain a routine with which you are comfortable. If there are young children, trying to maintain your sanity. Forcing yourself not to be critical (even in your thoughts) of a life-style of which you don't approve: their diet, the way they are raising the children, their parties, the housekeeping. Much too many things to have on your mind.

Whew! Sounds like a stressful life to me. I would rather spend my remaining years in my lovely apartment. I can handle the loneliness. It's a small price to pay for keeping my independence and being at peace.

Moving in with the children involves many considerations. If circumstances require you to do this, sit down and make yourself a list. Refer to it often. Establish a set of rules and promise yourself that you will abide by them. Nobody but you has to know about them. It won't be easy, but it's something you should do.

Promise yourself:

• I will consider my child's spouse in every way I can. I will try never to do anything that will cause him (her) to be unhappy because I am living in their home. I will never criticize my child's spouse to his (or her) face or behind his (or her) back.

• I will make sure, before I move in, that the financial arrangements we make are satisfactory to everyone. I will not be miserly with my money; neither will I lavish gifts and offers of financial aid, or try to buy their attention.

• I will find out beforehand what arrangements can be made for me to entertain my friends. I will let my family make the rules, and I will abide by them.

• If they don't attend church, I will make my own arrangements for getting there and back home. I will never say one word to them about their not going to church, and I will not leave my Sunday bulletins and Bible lying around as a silent hint.

• I will consider the Back Seat mine. No matter how I feel (and how right I know I am) about the way they are living their lives/raising their children/wasting their money/ruining their health, I will keep my thoughts to myself if it kills me.

It's best to live alone and maintain your independence for as long as you can. If you must live with one of your children, it can work—even be a happy solution—but only if you follow the rules.

CHAPTER 19:

Grandparenting

We hear a lot of talk about how it used to be for grandparents. They had more authority in the family; the grandchildren obeyed and respected them. Grandmothers ruled as matriarchs.

It's not like that today, and in many ways the change pleases us old ladies. We are much more independent, lead lives separate from our children and grandchildren, and most of us live alone and like it.

For the most part, we're happy, and although we love our grandchildren, we can stand to have them with us for only short periods of time. Two weeks is about tops. "Then I am very glad to send them home to their parents," we say.

We read about the good old days when grandparents were the center of the family, giving sage advice to their grown children and dispensing the wisdom of generations to their grandchildren. But just try giving advice to your grown children! It's true that we have some wisdom of generations to impart to our grandchildren, but few of them will stop long enough to listen to us.

In those good old days, the grandparents usually lived with their children and were handy for changing diapers, wiping runny noses, and calming the little storms that threatened. They helped with the housework and the cooking. They were full-time, live-in baby-sitters. When you contribute that much, you are entitled to give advice.

Today most of us don't live with our children. Many of us don't even live in the same state. We have become an extremely mobile society, and even though we tend to stay put, our children don't.

I have read articles recently bemoaning the fact that older members no longer have any emotional attachment to grandchildren or take any responsibility for them. Family ties and continuity are breaking. These articles contained no solutions, merely a sadness over the finding.

I'm not so sure it's a true picture. All of the grandparents I have talked to retain very strong emotional ties to their grandchildren. As a matter of fact, older people today have more time and more money to have fun with their grandchildren, to indulge them once in a while. They may not see them on a daily basis, but when they are with them, they lavish their love and attention on them.

We don't have any reason to feel sorry for the grandchildren of today. Most children past ten or twelve in the old days didn't have any grandparents. They died so much younger than we do nowadays.

Actually, grandparenthood is a relatively new thing. Many of us are still asking questions about it, casting around for some answers. Many of us who are still far from death already have great-grandchildren. The increase in the divorce rate has raised the problem of grandparents' legal rights. Not very long ago, this was unheard of.

In any case, a grandparent is still a vital part of a child's life, and the children are, of course, the bright jewels in any grandparent's life.

There are pillows, bumper stickers, posters saying, "Ask me about my grandchildren." There are Grandma's Brag Books to be filled with snapshots and drawings.

We raised our children to the best of our ability. We were busy and had to cope with cooking and housecleaning and shopping and hundreds of other things every day. Some of us worked at full-time jobs, too, and some of us raised our children alone. We wished there were time to play with our children, to lie in the grass beside them and talk about the clouds overhead. To dream with them and listen to them. However, there was precious little time for these things, so we packed school lunches, drove them to Girl Scout meetings, and cheered at Little League games. We loved them very much, but there wasn't much time left over for fun. Besides, our job was to teach and train them, to help them distinguish right from wrong, and too often we had to forgo the loving fun in order to be a proper parent.

That's all in the past. Now we have grandchildren and spare time and some discretionary income. We don't have the responsibility, and therein lies the difference. Without the responsibility, we can lavish our love on our grandchildren and listen to their dreams and talk to them and have some fun with them. We have much more to give now and can enjoy giving it.

Instead of being the respected but ignored white-haired matriarch in the corner, we can offer our grandchildren friendship.

Grandma today is probably wearing shorts or slacks and sports a swinging hairstyle and likes to do things and go places. Her tapered nails are shiny with color, and she moves in an aura of perfume. She takes her grandchildren swimming and hiking and engages in active pastimes.

The change in the American family life during the last thirty years is amazing. We old ladies can look back and remember how it was for us and how it is for our children and marvel at such profound changes as TV, air-conditioning, stereos, sliced bread, and an overall higher standard of living. Most of these changes came about after World War II, and part of the reason, perhaps the biggest reason, for the changing role of grandparents is simply the fact that we are living so much longer.

Also, the birth rate is declining. Whereas in the past, few children ever knew their grandparents, the children of the future will probably enjoy the love and attention of four grandparents well into adulthood.

It isn't all roses. As the old saying goes, it ain't been saucered and blowed yet. A few things remain to be ironed out, more to be learned as young and old adjust to this new phenomenon.

Old people intensely desire independence. Everyone in our family tried to get my ninety-eight-year-old father-in-law to give up his driver's license. Driving had become extremely unsafe for him and for others, but that driver's license was almost the last vestige of his independence, and he clung to it until the day he died. This wish is very important, and it must be considered and understood by anyone studying old people. Grandmas will no longer take on the role of baby-sitter in exchange for a corner of a house. They don't have to. Some of them won't even baby-sit for an evening.

At the same time, we want to maintain strong, meaningful ties with our families, and particularly with our grandchildren. The dilemma can be tough.

If you live a great distance from your grandchildren, your relationship is mostly symbolic. You represent something important to the children, but your presence is not possible. I am in this category. I seldom see my grandson, and even when we talk on the phone, I have to remind him, "This is your grandmother in Texas." I learned to do that the hard way. Some time ago I had to listen to a long, breathless conversation that was directed to a grandmother he knew and saw often. At last I cut in and identified myself, and the conversation went downhill from that point on.

We send cards and little gifts and remember them on birthdays and at Christmas. We cherish the notes that begin, "Dere Grandma," and that's about it. It can't be helped, and we must deal with reality. We opt to live in a warm climate where we will never again have to shovel snow, and our children live thousands of miles away. I heard of one grandmother who said, "My daughter lives on the other side of the country, where she is holding my grandchildren hostage."

The grandparents who live near or with their grandchildren have an entirely different set of problems. Even though I struggle with jealousy over grandparents who see their grandchildren nearly every day, I wonder if sometimes it isn't a bit much. I have heard grandparents say that the grandchildren drop in just as they have decided to take a nap, that they feel obligated to have home-baked cookies on hand, and that many parents are more than happy to have their children spend a night or a weekend with Grandma.

Most old people are neither of the above—far away from their grandchildren, or with them practically in their laps all the time. Most see their grandchildren often enough to become friends with them.

If you are lucky enough to be able to see your grandchildren on a fairly regular basis, that's wonderful.
Children need someone to listen to them, to pay attention to them. Older people are pretty much in the
same boat, so the two generations have something precious to offer each other.

The main thing all grandparents must learn and
practice is to mind their own business. Not interfering
seems to be the most difficult aspect of grandparenthood. You may know positively that certain methods
your daughter or son is using to raise children are
wrong. At the very least, you know a better way. You
absolutely must keep your opinions to yourself. Look
the other way; don't say one word. Even if it nearly
kills you. It's extremely difficult, I know. You have
been through all the things they are going through,
and you have learned so much by actual experience
that it hurts to see them making mistakes. Stay out of
it. This kind of meddling is the worst thing you can
do.

I remember how I felt when I was a child and my
mother scolded me and sent me to my room. Grandma
would intercept me in the hallway and whisper,
"You're not a bad girl. Grandma loves you. Here's a
piece of candy. Now, don't tell your mother." At that
moment, I loved my grandmother with all my heart.
I was very angry with my mother, and I went to my
room with my piece of candy feeling a little better.

For me, the child, having a grandmother like that

was wonderful. But I had been disobedient and shouldn't have had my pain eased with loving whisperings behind my mother's back. I can see now that it was extremely unfair to my mother. My grandmother had no right to interfere, and she caused arguments and hurt feelings between my parents until the day she died. The only reason her interference didn't cause more lasting effects was that she died several years before she reached the age of sixty.

We can't raise our grandchildren, or train them, but we can be their friends and listen to them and talk to them and have fun with them. We can teach them good things and tell them what it was like in the olden days. Children are fascinated with stories about the past. They ask, "If you didn't have TV, Grandma, what did you do?" And you tell them about the games you played as a child, Red Light and Kick the Can, and reading the Sunday funnies and about cars with running boards and rumble seats—things they know nothing about.

(This game can backfire, though. I was surprised once when my daughter came home from Sunday school on Palm Sunday and asked me if I had been able to touch Jesus when He rode into Jerusalem.)

As your grandchildren grow and begin college and marry and have babies, you can help with tuition costs and books and weddings. If you're smart about it and play your cards right and never interfere, you can play a large part in the life of your grandchildren and great grandchildren. You can leave behind some lovely memories.

During the years I was a church secretary, a group of people I loved and relied on were the volunteers. When I was swamped with work, which was quite often, I could always call some of them to come into the church office and stuff envelopes or type labels or get a newsletter ready for mailing. They were there when I needed them, but they never told me how to do my job. Grandparents should be like that.

The main thing we have to give is love. It's a love that is different from any we have ever experienced. This love is free of responsibility; we can just love our grandchildren and be their friend. The special love that grandparents have for their grandchildren is beyond explanation.

My grandmother, waylaying me in the hallway with a piece of candy and telling me that she loved me, had a very special love in her heart. However, we can show that love in a better, noninterfering way. We are going to be part of our grandchildren's lives for a long time, and will probably see them into adulthood. We have to do it right.

Expressing this full, free love in the proper way will keep us feeling young and will be a rich inheritance for our grandchildren.

CHAPTER 20:

Practice the Art of Listening

We love to talk, especially as we grow older and endure so many lonely hours. We start talking whenever we come across a warm body with ears. It's natural and understandable, but it would be advantageous to listen now and then. Sometimes the only thing we can do for a friend is to listen.

My son had been dating a sweet, intelligent young lady for several months. I liked her a lot. She was an independent soul and didn't stand for any nonsense from him.

Great, I thought. He has found a good woman. I was hearing wedding bells.

And then one day he told me it was all over. I wanted to know why, and he answered, "Well, it has been too much of a one-sided relationship. She could always sing her song, but I could never sing mine."

She didn't listen to him. And he got tired of it.

Most of us are hard of hearing. We don't really listen to others.

After my husband died I wanted to talk about him. I deeply needed to speak of him, to remember his face and his special ways.

Maybe it was because he was dead and all I had left were memories. Perhaps I was afraid that those precious memories would go just as quickly as he did and I would truly have nothing at all of him. Talking about him, remembering, would keep some part of him alive.

This wasn't a little wish, or a hankering; it was a deep, desperate longing within me.

Of course, no one let me do that. I know they meant well, but every time I tried to talk about my husband, to resurrect sweet memories of him, somebody changed the subject. They veered the conversation into other avenues.

They thought they were being good to me and sparing my feelings. They were sure they were protecting me. They were wrong.

One woman came to me in those first dark, confused days and said, "I know exactly how you feel!"

I looked at her through my tear-swollen eyes. She was old, and I was young. Her children were all grown and on their own. Mine were young, the youngest not even in school yet. She had enjoyed many years with her husband. We had only started on the first leg of our adventure together.

That woman ignited a flash of anger in me. "No,

you don't know how I feel. You don't have any idea of how I feel!" I almost yelled at her.

I hurt her feelings and later I apologized, but she had been wrong in making that statement. She hadn't been listening to me.

We must open up to others and listen to them. Sharing concerns is a necessary ingredient of friendship. There are the hopes that we would not dare talk about openly; the specific ambitions we have. We can talk about the things we have done that we have doubts about. We can unload some of our emotional hurts and pains. We can ask a friend to pray with us. Most of all, we can listen.

Particularly in our later years do we need compassionate, listening friends. We are alone so much of the time, reflecting and wondering behind the closed gates. Just to have someone listen to us once in a while, to hear what we have been thinking and pondering, is to open the doors and let in a breath of fresh air.

When I go to my friend to unburden my heart, I don't expect her to try to top me. And she never does. What she does is listen and sympathize and pray for me. I do not come to her for advice, and she seldom gives it. My friend comes to me in the same spirit and with the same expectations.

I know that I can go to my pastor with anything that is troubling my heart. But there are times when I don't want a pastor's response. I want my friend to put her arms around me and hold me for a minute or two and tell me that she understands. By clutching each other's hands, unashamed of our tears, we comfort each other.

I have learned a couple of things from all of this. The first thing I learned is not to be hard of hearing. Listen, I tell myself. Shut your mouth and listen!

I am so glad I learned that. Not long ago a dear friend's husband died. She was way up North and I was way down South, and it was impossible for me to go to her. But I wrote her a little note saying, "I remember him so well, and I loved him, too. If you feel like talking about him, call me."

Just before Christmas Eve, she called and we talked for an hour about her husband. We dredged up memories that were sweet to both of us and shed some tears and laughed. It was good to talk about him; and I'm sure it was especially comforting for her. She still had a part of her beloved with her as we exchanged those memories.

I say to all widows now, "If you want to talk about him, come over or call." In every single case, they take me up on the invitation.

Another thing I have learned is never to say, "I know exactly what you are going through," because I don't and never can. Instead, I tell them I am sorry and I ask if there is anything I can do for them. There may be something even better to do, but I don't know what it is yet.

Don't be hard of hearing! Most of us talk too much. Sometimes we talk so much, even God can't get through. We don't listen to what people are saying to us. Maybe all a person wants is a willing ear. Not advice, instruction, or even sympathy. He or she just needs someone to listen.

No matter how old you are, you can always lend an ear. There may be other oldsters who need to be listened to; there may be young people who need it, too.

So turn up your hearing aid and listen. Let somebody else sing her song.

How to Maintain a Right Attitude

CHAPTER 21:

Believe in Yourself

It's critical that we old ladies believe in ourselves. I don't mean that we are to believe we're smarter and wiser than the young people or that we are more pure of heart for having lived so many years. We'd only be fooling ourselves.

Every once in a while I hit it lucky and predict something that comes true, and my children look at me and say, "How did you know that was going to happen?" They think, at that moment anyway, that I am very wise. (I have done all I can to perpetuate that misconception.) The truth, of course, is that any moron who had lived as long as I have could have made the same prediction. I do not point that out to my children. If they believe that I am endowed with a mother's special sixth sense, who am I to contradict them?

For a long time I truly believed that when I told a lie, my mother knew it by the sudden blackened condition of my tongue. I don't blame my mother for using that trick. You do what you have to do.

Still, I remember well what I was like during my youthful years, and I was no better or no worse than the majority of young people today. I was different because the world was different then.

I experienced all the mean, petty feelings, the anger and frustration of youth. I didn't always make wise decisions or good judgments. I learned as I lived, often the hard way. I remember struggling with what I knew was right and what I really wanted to do.

St. Paul wanted more than anything to be a good person, the kind of person God wanted him to be, but he failed repeatedly, and it distressed him. Still, he kept on doing the things he hated, the things he didn't want to do, and he cried in shame, "Why am I like this? Why do I act this way?"

I am like that, too. I might have known that what I was doing was not right, but I did it anyway. Then I would berate myself for being so weak.

Well, thank God those stormy days of my youth are in the past! That's all over now. Right?

I'm afraid not. We old ladies face temptations, too. For the most part, they aren't the same temptations, but when we succumb to them, we have those familiar feelings of self-abasement.

I still get unreasonably jealous. (What is she complaining about? She still has her husband, doesn't she? Look at that silly woman with her grandchildren! So they live only a few blocks away; does she have to act like an idiot about it?)

I become angry over some imagined slight. (My daughter called her mother-in-law. Why didn't she call me?)

I have periods of depression. (Nobody cares whether I live or die, so why can't I just die?)

I do not want to indulge in these unlovely emotions, but I do.

We can know, as Paul knew, that we have a God who forgives and understands over and over. Regardless of the structure of your faith, your denomination (or no denomination), the regularity of your church attendance, we all have a God who loves us and reads our hearts.

As we grow older, we begin moving closer to God. Perhaps the reason for this is the fact that we have more time. We have relied on God all of our lives, but now we have the luxury of uninterrupted hours and it is comforting to use some of them for prayer and searching the Scriptures.

Also, we have time now to think about what kind of person we are. After all these years of living and striving, what have we become?

We seriously examine ourselves now, perhaps for the first time, searching for the real person we have become. We are not hampered by the outward signs of beauty. What we see is what we get.

Not a single one of us can look at our aging selves

and say, "Hey, what do you know? I have arrived at a state of perfection."

We see an old lady who is sometimes grouchy, self-indulgent, stingy. One who feels sorry for herself, is demanding, selfish, independent to the point of silliness. She complains about too many things nobody can do anything about, and she worries endlessly and vocally about her health and the state of her finances. One day she is afraid she is going to die, and the next minute she tells everyone who will listen that she wants to die now.

She criticizes everything the young people do and say and swears by all that is holy that she was a youthful paragon of virtue. Young people of today are going to hell in a handbasket, she tells them often, and she yearns for the good old days.

You are or have been perhaps one or more of the above at one time or another. I have been one or more of the above. The truth is, we will go on making some of the same mistakes as long as we live.

So what? It's no reason to hate ourselves, or feel that we are hopeless. Last week I complained to one of my children about how lonely I am. Her eyes glazed over and I hated myself for talking like that. So I won't do that again for a long time. I will do something else I shouldn't do. I keep on doing the things I don't want to do and failing to do the things I want to do.

We are the same frail humans we always were and we go on making mistakes, but we can feel good about ourselves. We do the best we can, we try to do better, we're taking care of ourselves, and we have a God who loves us. What more do we need?

The last time Flash and I were together, my daughter took pictures of us. When I showed them to Flash, snapshots of two old ladies with their arms around each other, smiling at the camera, Flash grinned.

"You know what, Jane?" she said. "We are a couple of beautiful old broads."

We are. We are too fat, wrinkles erode our faces, we're too mean at times, and stingy and crabby and self-indulgent, but not always. The high moments when we're all the things we want to be outnumber the other times. God loves us—that's a fact. It stands to reason that we can and should love ourselves.

CHAPTER 22:

Just Because It's Old Doesn't Mean It's Good

The older I get, the more I remember of the past. I can recall words and events of forty years ago with absolute clarity but sometimes can't for the life of me remember what I need at the grocery store.

It's all right. I enjoy looking back. Many of my memories are happy ones; some bring me a great deal of comfort. How I love getting together with a friend from "the old days" and rehashing memories!

My children, and most young people, don't understand this at all. Either they indulge me, or they change the subject. "Let's not dwell in the past, Mom."

I'm not dwelling in the past; I only like to visit it now and then. I enjoy remembering the good times we had and the frightening times we lived through. I can recall every stage of development my children went through, and I get a kick out of the memories.

I can tell you all about a certain person who was young and on tiptoes to meet life, and the fun she had and the mistakes she made. I'm talking about me and my first job and first boyfriend and the time I ran away from home and spent a snowy afternoon in a movie theater.

But I stop. The eyes of my children are glazed over with polite boredom. I must remember to indulge in nostalgia with people my age. It's great fun to travel down memory lane together.

We old ones talk on and on and don't bore each other. "I remember, during the Depression, having one slip and one pair of panties, and I didn't get a new set until those were rags."

"Oh yes, and one Sunday dress that hung in the closet all week. You wore it only on Sunday."

"I remember we used to go to the corner grocery store. There were no malls or supermarkets then."

"And when we paid the bill on Saturday, the grocer gave us a big bag of candy free."

"Remember . . ."

On and on we gab, and it's a delightful time for us. Sometimes I think young people should listen to us because we probably have something to teach them. But maybe not. Each generation is entitled to make its own mistakes and enjoy its triumphs in its own way. Still, our reminiscing about the past is part of our recreation. I believe it's healthful, and we should be left alone to indulge when we want to.

However, there is one area where I must not indulge myself in this way. I must not rely on the pet slogans and "religious" sayings of long ago. And I must not make the mistake of saying that everything was better in the "good old days."

If I do, I will be in a rut that can be hazardous to my spiritual health.

For example, we are asked to give so that people can eat. In the subtropical coastal town where I live, the cold winters of the north send many of the street people, the unemployed and the homeless, to us. We are asked to help these people and those who work in shelters for them.

One or two of the good church-going folk always say, "The Lord helps those who help themselves." This isn't even biblical, but these people who have stopped growing in their faith have been using that same sorry excuse for not giving for many years.

When there is talk of giving money to the church or to the homeless or the hungry, they tighten their lips and shake their heads. "The Bible says that money is the root of all evil. All the church ever does is beg for money." The Bible doesn't say that at all! The *love* of money is the root of all evil, the Bible says, and that's an entirely different matter altogether. (Read 1 Timothy 6:10)

We can't go on saying and thinking the same things over and over. The good old days were not necessarily better, only different.

Remember, sure. Memories are fine, especially if

we profit from them, but we are supposed to keep grow-ing and learning.

I have seen the bumper stickers that say, "I found it!" I don't like them at all. I usually mutter to myself, "Well, bully for you. I never lost it in the first place."

But maybe there is still something for me to find. If I open my heart and mind and become a learner again, I could discover untold treasures. Jesus said, "I have yet many things to say to you." If I can recapture the curiosity I had when I was young and stop being an old know-it-all, who knows what our Lord will yet reveal to me?

We have to examine our faith and our life and our way of thinking every now and then. Are we clinging to our beloved old-time religion, which means actually that we haven't had a new thought about it for years? Have we stopped growing? We just want it if it's old, if it belongs to the past.

On the TV show "20/20," Hugh Downs always closes by saying, "We're in touch, so you keep in touch."

God is saying that to us. He is in touch with us, with our lives and our hurts and our happy times. He is aware of what's going on in our world. He is always there, loving us, has always been there, and will go on being there forever. And He expects us to keep in touch with Him. Know what's going on. Keep growing regardless of how old you are. Everything else has long ago stopped growing in you, but don't let that happen to your faith.

Just because something is old does not mean that it is best. If we give it a try, no matter how long we live, there can be something new growing in us all our lives.

CHAPTER 23:

Love, Sex, Dating, Remarriage

Back in the 1800s most marriages didn't last much longer than thirty years because death ended them at that point. Today people are married for fifty, sixty, and even more years, and that makes us pioneers in the matter of long-term marriages.

When the young bride and groom stand at the altar and vow, "I do" and "Until death do us part," they are probably not thinking about fifty or sixty or more years of togetherness. In fact, some men, and a few women, seem to have the idea that the first fifteen years are for the struggles and raising children and making money. The last fifteen are to be enjoyed with someone else, preferably someone younger.

Even in the early 1900s couples didn't have many years together after the last child left home. The average life span in those days was not much beyond forty-five.

Our life span has been expanded, and for the first time in history we are a group of people doing what has never been done before. We are marrying, raising a family, and then looking at twenty to thirty more years of marriage. The next generation will live even longer than us and is watching us, seeing how we handle these years, observing the mistakes we make, trying to understand our successes. We are leading the way, and what we do and how we do it are important.

The one problem is that the average woman's life span is longer than a man's, so we have a lot of widows. There aren't enough men to go around for each of us to have one until we die.

We live longer, we enjoy good health, we have energy to enjoy life, and our mental faculties are sharp. The sex drive does not die as we grow old. There is no reason for our later years not to be exciting and fulfilling.

Some of us widows opt not to remarry. I was in my forties when my husband died, and I had four young children to raise. I did not want to bring another Daddy into their lives, and I truly did not have the energy or time to cope with dating. By the time my children were on their own, I was so independent, so used to managing my own life, I didn't even consider marriage. Besides, at my age, there were two important considerations: I would have to be an exceptional old lady to fight the stiff competition and find the kind of man I would want. Second, if I did get a man, he would be old like myself, and I had no desire to live with an old man.

E. Jane Mall

I am sometimes jealous of old couples still together after many years, but there are also some I don't envy at all. I know a woman my age who is about to go crazy because of her husband. They have raised their children, and she tells of good years when they were both busy and productive and happy. They planned ahead, and there was ample money for a comfortable old age. However, the day her husband retired from his job, he also retired to his bed. And to the chair in front of the TV. He moves from one foot to the other with a slow, shuffling walk. He sighs a lot, doesn't talk much, and eats way too much. His wife figures they have possibly another fifteen to twenty years left, and she doesn't know how she is going to make it and keep her sanity.

Some widowed women—and women whose husbands have decided they want to live with someone else for the last twenty years—are not content to live without a man. They have a special problem.

Society is filled with young single women, and when this woman, who has experienced twenty years or more of marriage, who is still thinking of dating as it was for her twenty years ago, dares to go out and try her wings, it's a great shock.

The world is almost too different to comprehend. We can react with such a sense of shock that we run home and close our doors and refuse to have any part of it. And thus cut ourselves off from what we really want. Or we can plunge in and try to become a part of this new wave and find ourselves so perplexed and so at war with what we have always believed that we don't know where we stand.

Most of us have been raised to believe that certain things are wrong. Our guide is the Bible, and we have lived by its precepts and commandments.

However, if you watch TV, especially the soap operas, you can blow your mind. Does anyone really go to bed with anyone they're attracted to? Is that the way it really is out there?

Talk to your children; ask them to tell you honestly what it's like for dating couples nowadays. I did, and my kids said, "Okay, Mom, if you really want the truth, I'll tell you. It's a jungle."

It's a jungle, all right. Singles bars are a place to meet other singles. The so-called experts say that you can meet other singles in the church, at bowling alleys, and supermarkets. The trouble is, most of the men you meet in church are married. The men you meet in bowling alleys are with a mate or a date. Besides, would you go to a bowling alley alone, or with another old lady? Probably not. You could wander the aisles of a supermarket until you were one hundred years old and not meet a man who would offer to take you out to dinner.

So where does the single go? The answer over and over is "To a singles bar." Which is something we never heard of before.

In a singles bar, sex has the top priority. It's in

the air, all around you. Men and women meet and talk to each other, dance, shoot pool, but their eyes never stop moving. They are looking the others over, making sure they're not missing a better bet. You see couples meeting, talking a few minutes, and then leaving together. Sometimes they go to her place, sometimes to his, and sometimes to a car or van in the parking lot.

No flowers and candy, no phone calls, no going out to dinner. That's the way it is, and if you can't accept that, don't go to the singles bars.

The people in the singles bars, especially the men, are there for sex; make no mistake about it. I have talked to both men and women who frequent singles bars, and they agree. One man told me, "I go to them for sex, and usually get it. When I want to meet someone with a lasting relationship in mind, I do not go to singles bars."

I talked to a woman who went to singles bars, but she was not interested in sexual contact. She wanted to get out, to be with men, to have a good time one night a week. After a few tries, she had to give up. "If you don't want sex," she said, "you don't belong in a singles bar."

In many singles bars drinks are free for the ladies. This ploy is to bring them in, so that the men will have women to meet. Singles bars are called "meat markets." If you can shift your gears, and change your thinking, and this kind of sexual activity is okay with you, then the singles bar is where you should go. However, a word of warning: Because of AIDS, even the young singles are becoming very cautious.

I have painted a rather dark, frightening picture; that was my intention. Sad to say, it's a true picture. Many of the young people of today regard sex in a way we can't understand. I can't begin to understand where they got the idea that this is right and that they have the right to force this attitude on the rest of us. I would not like to see a generation of old ladies deciding to swim in this stream. I can't see it happening. If this makes me an old-fashioned fuddy-duddy, so be it.

Still, there are many women who are fifty and over who are without husbands for one reason or another and are lonely and want male companionship. What are they supposed to do? Some women want sex, but are appalled at the idea of looking for it from strangers at a bar. "Your place or mine?" is not in their vocabulary.

After twenty or more years of marriage, then suffering the agonies of a death or divorce, getting back into the social world is frightening, if not terrifying. We don't know how to do it. Some of us approach it with a sense of desperation, and some give up and retreat to the lonely life.

How about convincing yourself that it's not a matter of life and death, that you are going to make your life as enjoyable as possible, that you are not going to sit at home and feel sorry for yourself? Start looking into other possibilities, things you enjoy doing. You have spent many years pleasing others: now it's time to please yourself. Ask yourself what you want in life, what will truly please you, then go for it. Don't worry or think about what might happen, or whom you might meet; just enjoy yourself.

It's not going to be easy. You have spent so many years pleasing your husband and your children, you don't know how to live just pleasing yourself. But once you adopt this new attitude, you will have a better time, won't be so anxious. I have a friend who says, "No, I won't do that. It doesn't please me." That is a wonderful attitude for us old ladies to have. If it doesn't please you, don't do it. You have earned the right to say that.

Get out, join groups who are doing things that please you, and don't allow yourself to be caught up in activities that don't please you. Acquiring this attitude will take some doing, but you will have to do it. It will be your salvation. You may go on for the rest of your life, enjoying these things you're doing and never meeting a man to spend your life with. Well, what can I say? There is a shortage of men, and you might not be one of the lucky ones. But you will still have changed your attitude; you will have learned to please yourself and have some fun. You will be better off than if you lived a life of anxious desperation and seclusion.

However, you may be fortunate and meet a man

who asks you out on a date. You who have not dated for many years! If the man is around your age, he remembers what dating was like years ago, and that will help a lot. I have heard young people say that they hate dating. "It's the pits!" They don't know each other, don't know what to talk about; they wonder if the other person is disappointed in them. That's why going steady is so popular. This could be the experience of old ladies, too, and for that reason it would be wise to join a group of like-minded people and hope to meet your man there. Join a bird-watcher group or a bridge club, for instance, and from the start you have something in common.

If you are an old lady, embarking once again on the dating experience, it is very important that you please yourself. Don't look at each dating experience as some great big decision for your life. It's something to do, that's all. It's an opportunity to be with a man and enjoy yourself. If it doesn't work out, doesn't please you, that's the end of it. It is no great tragedy.

Base your acceptance of a man on your needs, and this will give you a sense of security that you never knew in your youth. After all your years of marriage, plus the grief experience of death or divorce, you should know pretty well what pleases you and what doesn't please you.

A widow friend of mine, in her eighties, was asked on a date by an elderly widower she had known for many years. They went out for dinner, attended concerts, and enjoyed each other's company. Once in a while, after a movie or concert, she would invite him in for homemade cake or cookies and a cup of coffee.

Then one night, as he was leaving, he said, "I think you should call me once in a while, instead of me always calling you for a date."

She responded, "I will never do that. I was not raised that way. Women do not ask men for dates."

And that was the end of the friendship. To this day she has never seen him again. And she doesn't care. It did not please her to do as he asked, and that was that. I suspect that he doesn't care very much either. He was pleasing himself. Perhaps he met a woman who was willing to call him for a date now and then.

The point is, you know what pleases you and what doesn't, and there is no sense in your doing things or putting up with things that don't please you. Not anymore. You are not that desperate, as youth can be desperate. You can afford to be flexible and accept or reject new attachments based on your own needs and desires.

A word of caution: Make sure that the things that please you aren't some form of self-indulgence or nostalgia that doesn't make much sense today. For example, it would be foolish to continue making pie crusts and biscuits with lard rather than with a vegetable shortening, wouldn't it? Yet I do know a woman who does this because "my mother's pie crusts and biscuits were the flakiest in the world. She used lard and it pleases me to use lard." One can't help but wonder how flaky she is.

It may please you to visit your husband's grave every Sunday with fresh flowers. However, if this means that one of your children must spend an hour or so picking you up, buying flowers, driving out to the cemetery, bringing you back home, aren't you simply being selfish?

My children are always telling me about new and different ways of doing things, of approaching new ideas, and it isn't always easy for me to listen to them and accept their ideas. (Look what my son has done to my casserole!) Still, some of their ideas are good ones. Of course, there are some tried-and-true beliefs we cling to, and rightfully so. However, be open to new ideas, new challenges, different ways of looking at things. You know it's right and necessary that you do this. If that attitude hadn't prevailed before, we wouldn't have the telephone or TV or sliced bread! You may not agree with many of the new attitudes and ideas, but at least open your mind and listen.

Define the things that please you; ask yourself if they still make sense, if you should implement some changes. Is your way the only way? Be open to new ideas, and don't be afraid to take chances. If you are emotionally healthy and mature, it won't be the end of the world if one of your choices is wrong.

Many old ladies have found great happiness in

marriages the second time around. Many have never married at all. It doesn't make any difference. All of us, married or not, can have happy, productive lives as long as we look within ourselves and to God for happiness. Accept the things that truly please you and avoid the things that don't. This sort of contentment isn't dependent on others.

CHAPTER 24:

Never Lose Hope

Sometimes I feel as if there is no hope for me. Just a mere fifteen years ago I went on a calorie-counting diet and lost thirty-five pounds. It took three months, but the pounds melted away and I felt great. Recently I went on the same diet, and I have lost exactly five pounds in three months! What's the use of trying?

I have been told that the reason I can't lose weight as easily as I did fifteen years ago is because everything has slowed down. Fifteen years ago I was working full-time. I was very active. Now I'm not.

I'm sure that is part of it, but another part of it is that I figure nobody cares how I look. I am sixty-eight years old; I don't have to try so hard anymore. Besides, there just isn't any hope left.

I keep forgetting that there is always hope. Sometimes hope is a desperate yearning. It's like the mesquite with its twisted, thorny branches reaching in all directions in a crazy sort of way. I do that. I look to this solution and to that answer to satisfy a deep, hungry yearning inside.

At other times my hope is more like a cat, crouched behind a chair, muscles taut, ready to spring at the first thing that moves. It doesn't matter that the first thing that moves is a silly ball of yarn: I pounce.

I surrender to futility too often these days. It's as if I am caught in a web and it's too hard to try to fight my way out.

I look at too many things in that same manner. I will never be pretty again, never slim, and my hair will never again be thick and glossy.

Then I stop and think. Hey, I am a Christian old woman, not just an old woman. And I am called to be different. To put different values on everything.

We live in the middle of futility. . . . Old age does that to us. I get so angry because I can't do many of the things I did so easily when I was young. I am not happy when I look into the mirror and see the wrinkles I have stopped counting. The fleshy throat and all the parts of me that sag are not pleasing.

I want to hang a picture on the wall. That requires getting the hammer and nail and the step stool and climbing up and pounding a nail in the wall. When I was young, I would do a simple job like that without giving it a thought. Now I hope the stool is strong and steady; I hope I don't fall. I am very cautious and careful. It annoys me to have to think so much about a simple little task.

Still, my hope should be intensified. Because I am a Christian, and that makes me different. Even in the midst of a dark world that sometimes shocks me. There are things in this world now that I never thought about when I was young. The appalling, terrifying world of drugs that is touching so many; young people living together, opting for no commitment; absolute trash on TV touted as entertainment. Sometimes I feel like huddling down within myself. I feel so helpless!

And yet there is a ray of hope. Every time someone praises God . . . every time one person gives in love to another . . . each time someone teaches a little one . . . there is hope. Hope is all around us because of the people we know and love and admire. Of course there is a rainbow round the corner!

Not long ago my daughter hugged me, and then she stepped back and said, "Mom, you have shrunk!"

We measured, and sure enough, I had shrunk by almost an inch. I was dismayed. After all, I was only five foot three to begin with!

Then I relaxed. Maybe there is less of me, and what is left is too fat and sagging and unlovely in some ways, but there is still hope for me. It's in my mind and my heart and in the fact that I won't give up. Every single day is worth living, worth looking forward to. I will believe, with hope in my heart, that I can make some small contribution for good to the day ahead.

CHAPTER 25:

Build Your Confidence and Destroy Your Fears

For many years I had to concentrate most of my energies on just getting by. Whether I liked it or not, I had to be at the office every day, and I had to be efficient, or I would be fired. I had children who required a roof over their heads and food and clothing. I had to take care of them and love them and nurture them until they grew up. I had a house to clean and take care of, laundry to be washed, a car to keep running, and groceries to buy.

I also had to make time for being with my children in a way that would help them know about love and faith. I had to teach them good things.

I was a very busy woman, and there were a lot of times when I would stop for a minute or two and think about the day when I would be able to "take it easy."

That day is here, and it has thrown me for a loop. I absolutely was not prepared for old age. I am afraid! Afraid of being too old, of course, and afraid of being sick and helpless. Afraid of breaking something that will make me even more helpless. Afraid of being so alone that I speak into the silence just to hear the sound of my own voice. I am afraid my money will run out and I will be poor and dependent. That's what old age has done to me. It has filled me with fears.

Some of my fears have been realized. I fell against a steel desk one morning and injured my knee and tore some ligaments. In addition to the pain, I couldn't walk, and I had some weeks of learning what it would be like to be helpless in that way.

And my loving children, who once enjoyed my company, and took me out to lunch, and came home begging for my cooking, disappeared. It seemed like one day they were with me and the next they had all gone somewhere. For a while it was devastating, and I felt very sorry for myself. I adjusted, but only because I had no choice.

Most of our fears are needless. All in the head. Remember when your children were teenagers, out at night, driving the car? Remember the nights when they didn't come home when they were supposed to and they didn't call?

Remember how you paced, how your heart thumped? Worry. Fear. How many times did you look out the window expecting to see a patrol car pull up? If the phone had rung, you would have jumped completely out of your skin. Your imagination worked overtime.

By the time your teenager walked in with a big

smile, you were ready to collapse. Later, you had to admit to yourself that all your worrying had been for nothing. It certainly didn't do anybody any good, least of all you.

Fear can make you ill. Really physically ill. Sustained fear can shorten your life. It can prevent you from doing what you want to do. Whether it's real fear (it usually isn't) or whether it's an imagined fear (it usually is), it can hurt you.

Long ago, imagined fears kept you from going to bed at your usual hour and getting a restful sleep. You could have done that, as you later discovered, but your fears kept you awake and pacing the floor.

The only way to rid ourselves of our fears is to take some kind of action.

I have a friend named Patsy who is a lovely old lady. One day we were talking about our fears, and she said that one fear had sort of plagued her most of her life. She was afraid of the water. Going into a lake or swimming pool was not a pleasant experience because of her fear of the water.

Now, your reaction might very well be: So what? You're old; surely you can manage to stay away from lakes and swimming pools for the rest of your life.

But Patsy wanted to conquer this fear, so she took swimming lessons. The class was for old people, and Patsy said, "I didn't feel out of place at all! There were all those sagging stomachs and flabby arms in the pool, and I felt right at home."

Gradually, Patsy overcame her fear of the water. I will never forget the day she came to me and said, "Jane, I jumped into the pool! I jumped in! The instructor let me hold my nose, but I jumped into the deep end!"

Patsy took action and she rid herself of a fear. Perhaps that doesn't sound like such a big deal to some, but I admire Patsy greatly.

Use your head. Some fears are real, but most of them are not. If you have a fear, do something about it, conquer it, and then forget it.

I read about an old lady in another state who trembled every time she heard about a rape. She lived alone, and she was afraid of this happening to her.

Still, she always left her bedroom window open at night because she insisted she couldn't sleep unless she had fresh air to breathe.

A man crawled into her bedroom one night and raped her.

She had a very real fear, but she refused to take a necessary precaution.

It's too bad that we live in a world where this sort of thing happens, but we must face facts whether we like them or not.

I, too, am afraid of being raped, as is any woman. And I prefer a room filled with fresh air when I sleep. But my bedroom windows are locked when I go to bed, and I don't roam the streets after dark.

I am afraid of falling and breaking a bone that

won't heal. Of course I am. But I walk carefully and take a calcium supplement. I'm going to do everything I can to prevent that particular fear from becoming a reality.

When I owned a car, I was afraid of driving on the expressway. I knew that I was very nervous and would probably cause an accident, so I didn't drive on the expressway. It's as simple as that. I could go anyplace I wanted to go by traveling the side streets. It took longer, but I had all the time in the world. The point is, I eliminated one fear from my life.

People are profiting from our fears. I read that medical frauds make at least ten billion dollars every year. These people tell us about their magic cures for arthritis, for cancer. They sell pills and creams guaranteed to restore our youth. They know what we're most afraid of and feed on our fears. Surely we have lived long enough so that we are smarter than they are. By conquering our fears, we can put these crooks out of business.

Try to conquer every little fear you have. Patsy could certainly have ignored her fear of the water, but by conquering it she gained a lot of self-confidence. And that measure of self-confidence will help to keep other fears at bay.

In order to rid myself of my fear of the expressway, I had to take an alternate route. That wasn't a matter of giving in to my fear. I knew that I could easily cause an accident, and as long as I could go another route,

I put one fear out of my life. There will usually be an alternate route for us to take.

I don't believe that God wants us to be frightened, cringing old ladies. He doesn't want us to be dominated by our fears, or falling for the quacks who promise us impossible things. We are nearing the end of a wonderful journey, and we are fools if we travel in fear.

In the Bible we read: "Let not your heart be troubled: ye believe in God, believe also in me. In my father's house are many mansions: if it were not so, I would have told you. I go to prepare a place for you." (John 14:1–2)

It is all going to turn out the way it's supposed to turn out. And I am not to allow my heart to be troubled or worn down with fear.

If it weren't true, He would have told us so!

Those are comforting words, and we can take them to our hearts.

It's going to be all right. We don't have to be troubled and afraid. God is taking care of things, and if that weren't true, He would have let us know.

How You Can Prepare for Death

CHAPTER 26:

Living in the Past

The older we get, the more we enjoy reminiscing, and we should be allowed to indulge in it without any criticism. Sometimes the remembering is so painful that we can't hold back the tears. That's all right. Some pain and sorrow are a part of the life we have lived; those times are woven in with the good and happy times.

I am not talking about leaning on your memories or using them in order to avoid what's really going on in your life. This is a sad way to go, and we don't want to do that. We don't need to do that if we're living life to the fullest and accepting its daily challenges.

Our final years have more significance for us when we recall the years that led up to them. We can't dismiss what we were, how we strived, and how our dreams and hopes and ambitions came out. How and why they didn't come out as we planned is important, too.

Our memories can be comforting because they represent our life. We can take pleasure in the victories, and know that we are wiser because of the failures. We can't do anything about them—they are only memories of what has already happened—but they are important to us. As our independence fades, we can still remember ourselves as vital, alive, young adults facing life on tiptoes, ready for anything that happened our way.

We know we can't recapture those years—we aren't trying to do that—but to relive and review them in our memory is pleasant. As long as we don't use our memories as a weapon, we should be left alone to indulge in them whenever we want to.

If we continually insist that everything was better years ago, and that young people of our generation had more strength, moral purity, good sense, and loyalty than the young of today, no one is going to listen to us. Nobody cares that you walked ten miles to school, in the snow, with no shoes.

However, if we can talk about our struggles and our fears and our mistakes and say to our children and grandchildren, "This is what I did and it turned out fine. It was the right thing to do" or "I made a mistake. I should have handled it like this. I see now . . ." your memories can help you teach them good things.

If our children and grandchildren will listen, they can catch a spirit of continuity, to help them tie it all together by knowing where they came from, who their ancestors were. When you tell your grandson, "Your great-grandfather was a train engineer, and in those days . . ." you are telling him about a part of yourself, and about a way of life that has ceased to exist. He can read about trains in books, and of coal being shoveled to make them run, but how wonderful to learn of these things by the telling of how his own great-grandfather did them!

Many young people have little patience with our reminiscing. They act almost as though we're feeble-minded for doing it, but I believe it's a healthful pastime. As long as we don't get too self-indulgent or use our memories as a yardstick against today's youth, our trips to the past can be profitable for them and for us.

We know that we are nearing the end of life; we have lost many things, many people: and we can feel our independence fading like a wisp of steam. Our memories help us see the significance of our lives as a whole. We can look at the things we accomplished, the raising of our children, the love we gave, the help we offered, and know that even though we did those things because we wanted to, they do mean something. They add up to some kind of a total. We may not have amassed a fortune, or ever felt the rays of fame turned on us, or did anything the world considers significant and important, but our lives have been significant to us and to a handful of people.

Remembering the past, and integrating it with the present, can be meaningful for you and for your children and grandchildren.

If you can get a little organized in your remembering, you will be amazed at the memories that will pop up in your mind. We have clear memories of a world without TV or Kool-Aid or shopping malls or credit cards. Tell city children about farm life. A country church, a drug store with a marble counter and little round tables and wire chairs. The ice man delivering blocks of ice, swimming in a big hole in a pasture, and how your mother made yellow bars of soap during the war years. I saw thorn apples on sale in the exotic foods department of a supermarket the other day; memories of walking through a sea of them made me smile.

Many of the memories of our lives are sweet (a few sad), but all of them are important—what brought us to today. Dredge them up and offer them, in a loving way, to your grandchildren. They won't forget all of them: and they will learn from a few of them. Then, when you are gone, some of the memories will remain and will be handed down.

CHAPTER 27:

The Need to Prepare for Death

The closer I move toward the day of my death, the angrier I become. Not with the inevitability of death, but with the people who refuse to call a spade a spade.

"He passed away."

"I lost her two years ago."

"God took him."

Why in the world can't we say, "He died"? Or "She is dead"? I feel like responding:

"How did he pass? Did he float?"

"You lost her? You have only lost someone when you don't know where they are. Don't you know where she is?"

"God didn't take him. Let's hope God received him."

But I let it go. We love to trick ourselves by saying our loved ones passed on or were lost or taken. Perhaps it eases the pain inside that comes from knowing that they died.

The thing is, from the moment of birth, death is

a fact of life. And there isn't anything to be so afraid of. By skirting around the edges of what really happens, we find ourselves unprepared for our own death. Eventually, and certainly, the day is going to come when we will discover that we don't pass away or get lost or taken. We die. I prefer to face that fact now and be as prepared for it as possible. This is our final stage of life. It is inevitably going to lead to death, which is the natural end of life. What else? Do you want to live forever? I know I don't. Imagine getting older and older, and all that goes with it, and not being able to die. We hope that we can remain healthy, able to care for ourselves, independent. We don't know what lies around the corner, but we hope. The only certainty is our death; and we can prepare ourselves for it.

When my father-in-law had almost reached his one-hundredth birthday, he died. He was ready to die, and he had lived such a long, saintly life that he could accept his death calmly. There was no need for a lot of tears and mourning at his funeral. We were well aware that our tears were for ourselves, not for him. It was so natural. He lived a long, productive life, he grew very old, and then he died.

We go through our stages of life. From infancy to Daddy's little girl, young lady, bride, mother, and grandmother. We have lived through them. They came and we knew they were coming and we accepted some, welcomed some, and coped with others.

Death is another stage of life, the most certain one. Absolutely inevitable.

You may not have married; you may not have been a mother. You probably have known some who didn't even grow old. But none of us can escape the final stage of life. Doesn't it make sense to prepare for it?

I remember how impatient my daughters were to cross the line and become teenagers; they couldn't wait to start menstruating, begin to date, get married, have a baby. They knew these things were going to happen, and they prepared themselves as much as possible for them.

Even though it doesn't sound like much of a fun thing, it's time we start to prepare ourselves for our death. If we do, we will remove the fear and perhaps, in the doing, teach young people some good things.

For most of us, growing old has taught patience. We have learned over the years that certain things are going to happen; our fretting and fussing and growing angry don't make any difference.

A baby is going to be born; a sick person will recover; a loved one will die. When the time comes, it will happen. We wait for good news with impatience, and we wait for bad news with dread. No matter how we wait, it happens.

We finally know that Scripture is right: to every thing there is a season.

To every thing there is a season, and a time

to every purpose under the heaven. A time to
be born, and a time to die; a time to plant,
and a time to pluck up that which is planted.
(Ecclesiastes 3:1-2)

All along the way we see signs of death. So many
of our friends are dead.

That older woman I loved so much when I was a
young woman: she died years ago.

The teacher who guided me through the maze of
learning and taught me how to spell: dead for many
years.

The pastor who was my rock of strength for so long:
he died a few years ago.

On and on it goes, these reminders that I, too,
will have to die.

Some died beautifully with a smile, ready to go.
Others I have known left this life kicking and screaming and crying about the injustice of having to die
before they were ready.

Some suffered before they were released; some
shook their fists at God; some begged to be allowed
to die; and some were taken by surprise, dying before
they woke up.

I have been wondering about myself and how I
will handle my death. I hope it doesn't take me by
surprise, but I guess it really won't matter. Mainly, I
don't want to leave a void.

My children and friends will have pictures of me

to look at. But they will have pictures of me at my fifth birthday party, at age eighteen, as a bride, at forty and fifty and on. They will be looking at pictures of a lot of different people, and not one of them will be who I was at the time of my death. It's possible that someone will take my picture minutes before I draw my last breath, but neither that picture nor any of the others will reveal who I really was. A picture can't do that.

I want to be remembered for what I have been inside and how I lived and how I died.

Perhaps my life hasn't added up to all that much. In fact, I know it hasn't. The older I get, the more I think about my accomplishments. I think about what I will leave behind to fill the space I took up for so long.

I look at the signs of death: I accept the fact that the time is coming for me.

I am coming to the truth that the parts of me that will live on are the acts of love that I have performed, the warm smiles I have given, the patient understanding, the kind deeds.

My study is filled with bookshelves. And on some of the shelves are the books that I have written. They are in English, Swedish, German, Chinese, and African dialect. I think it's very impressive. I do have something to leave behind. After I am dead my children can point to those books and say, "My mother wrote those."

Then I stop and think. My children have not read all my books! They grew up thinking all mothers came equipped with typewriters. They couldn't tell you the titles of all of my books any more than they can recite the names of the seven Dwarfs. Well, I give the Dwarfs better odds than I do my books.

My children grew up with a mother who stopped typing long enough to hand them a cookie or to kiss a sore knee. They have always taken my writing for granted. It's what their mother did. I feel that my books are an important accomplishment in my life. My children don't.

My son remembers the time when he did something he should not have done. "You never rejected me because of that, Mom. You still loved me and supported me, and I will never forget that."

My daughter tells me, "I love you, Mom. I need you in my life because I know how much you love me."

Well, of course! They are my children, and of course I love them. What's so great about that?

I look at my family photo album and my shelf of books and even my antique furniture and pieces of silver and the money in my bank account. All of the material things I have to leave my children. And it dawns on me that all of these things could be stolen or burned today. There has to be something indestructible for me to leave behind.

I know what that something else is: my love for them; my absolute acceptance of what they have become; my inexhaustible patience with their rebellious ways; the Christian example I tried to be for them. These are the things I leave for them, and nobody can take them away.

And so we grow old and we learn and we come to terms with our death. The waiting isn't always easy. Sometimes we wish we could put it off indefinitely; other times we wish it would hurry up. However we feel, it will happen when it is time for it to happen.

I find a lot of comfort now in knowing that the end will not take me by surprise. I may be alive one minute and dead the next, but it will not take me by surprise. Because I am preparing for my death by being more loving and kind and gentle. I am trying on a daily basis to be more the kind of person that I'm supposed to be. I have plenty of time now to lavish love and understanding; to listen to someone who needs to talk; to help others in some small ways.

It's what I have to leave behind. Instead of listing my achievements, or counting my money or possessions, I can make sure that the memories of me will be sweet and in some way instructive.

My mother told me about a barrel of dishes she found after her mother died. She didn't want the old things and put them out for the trashmen to pick up. Later, she was told by a relative that those dishes had belonged to her great-grandmother and had been passed down, through the generations. They were meant to be a precious legacy, but they became trash.

How often have you heard about some young person inheriting a lot of money and squandering every cent?

It is very important for us to think about what we are leaving behind.

- If you're cranky and complaining, improve your disposition.
- If you expect your children to wait on you and worry about you, get real! Work at being independent.
- If you're wallowing in your loneliness, get out in the world and talk to someone.

Envision a different picture of yourself, one that is going to remain in people's minds after you're dead. Right now it's in your power to make that picture what you want it to be.

Finally, erase your fears of death; accept it as another stage of life. You have lived long, dear lady. You have endured so much; you can handle it! We don't know when the Master of the house will arrive, but we can prepare our minds and souls for the reception.

CHAPTER 28:

Write Your Will

Since the beginning of time, brothers and sisters have argued and fought and even killed over an inheritance. They are still doing it today.

I like the attitude of the old lady who said she was going to spend all her money before she died. I don't know if she did that or not, but even if she did, her children would find something to fight over.

No matter how much or how little you own, you have a responsibility to write a will. Your possessions may not be worth much money, but when you die, these things will suddenly acquire a great symbolic value. At least, enough to fight over.

There can be fights and arguments so bitter, the rifts will never heal. The arguments are usually way out of proportion to the value of the possessions. Many horror stories float around about brothers and sisters not speaking to one another for years because one of them got mother's silver service.

Old people sometimes use their wills to manipulate

their children, threatening to change their will every time the children don't please them.

Some exist without everything but the bare necessities so that they can leave money to their children.

Some give while they are alive, saying they don't want the children to have to wait until they die for their inheritance. Also, they get a lot of pleasure out of making the children happy.

I knew a wealthy lady who called her two daughters to her home. They divided up all the woman's jewelry. They amiably spent a whole afternoon. You can have this ring if I can have this locket.

She let them talk it out and decide alone. When they were satisfied with the distribution, lists were made, and she later wrote their preferences into her will. In the meantime, she kept her jewelry and wore it and enjoyed it. That sounds like a good idea for all of us. Call the children in and let them decide what they want, what is fair, and write it down and incorporate it into your will. If they change their minds after you're dead, and fight, it's their problem, not yours.

I don't have much of worth, and the few pieces I have, I hope my children will cherish. I have written a brief history of the special things. A table that is over one hundred years old: "This was your great-grandmother's table. It is over one hundred years old. Your grandmother and I carried it two miles from the farm to the railroad station when I was twelve years old." I taped this to the underside of the table. I did this with all the special pieces, and I have told the children to look there, to refresh their memory. They have chosen the pieces they want, and this is written in my will. Any money I have will be divided equally.

It is difficult to believe, but the statistics say that only about three out of every ten of us die with a valid will. I suspect that many people feel that they don't have much to leave, so why write a will? Remember, it takes very little for people to fight over! And you certainly don't want all your worldly possessions distributed by the state.

The best thing to do is have a lawyer draw up your will so that you can be sure it's legal. If you don't have much money or don't want to spend a lot on this, use one of the legal clinics that can be found in many cities. They will draw up a simple will for around fifty dollars. Perhaps you qualify to have your will drawn up free by your state senior legal services office.

Lawyers charge by the hour, so it would be a good idea to write your will as completely as possible before you go to the lawyer's office. No special format is required, so merely write it in simple language. State the date and your name. Choose a person to be your executor. This can be one of your children, a banker, or a friend. Talk it over with this person beforehand and be sure he or she is willing to act in this capacity. It will be up to the executor to inventory all your assets, pay any of your debts, plus your funeral expenses, and distribute your assets according to your wishes as stated in your will. Write everything down, in paragraphs, then take this information to your lawyer to have it written in proper legal form. Remember that each state has its own rules and regulations for writing a valid will, so you may have to write a new one if you move.

If there is a relative who would automatically inherit a percentage of your estate, and you don't want this relative to inherit anything, that will have to be stated.

As you figure your assets (home, car, life insurance, furniture, jewelry, savings accounts, etc.), you will probably be surprised at how much you're worth. Your liabilities (loans, credit card and department store balances, etc.) will probably be the lowest they have ever been.

I talked it over with my children first, and I was in for a few surprises. I had no idea that my daughter, who has been away from home for so many years, felt any attachment to my furniture. "Mom, if you don't leave that one table to me, I will really be hurt." We ironed out all those details together before I took my notes to the lawyer.

No matter how much you have, or how little you think you have, you do not want these things to be a basis for arguments and hurt, bitter feelings after you die.

The best thing to do is to talk to your children now. Ask them if there is something that they would particularly like to have. See how the others feel about it. Let them argue a little now, with you as moderator. It will go much more smoothly than it will later, with the pain of your death enlarging everything out of proportion.

You have plenty of time, so why not make a list of the things that must be done when you die? Number them, provide names and addresses and policy numbers, your Social Security number, and so forth. Address envelopes to all who must be contacted, with instructions on what to do. "Enclose policy and death certificate and mail immediately." It will be a big help to your children; and you can be sure that they will receive all the benefits to which they are entitled.

CHAPTER 29:

Some Thoughts
About Dust

In the order of the burial of the dead, it says, "We therefore commit his body to the ground: earth to earth, ashes to ashes, dust to dust."

And, in the garden of Eden: "Dust thou art, and unto dust shalt thou return." (Genesis 3:19)

Well! I don't like that very much. I have fought a battle with dust for all of my adult life. I have twirled up little cyclones of dust day after day as I swirled my dust cloth over the tops of furniture.

It never did much good. No matter how often I dusted, it was all right back there the next day.

Sometimes I would rebel and give the dusty furniture a dirty look as I walked through the rooms of my house. Those were the times when later I would read sweet messages written in the dust by a loving husband. A heart drawn with a forefinger, or "I love you" scrawled in the dust on a tabletop. Then I was able to dust with a smile on my face.

Now that I am older, and alone, and have few visitors, I don't dust the furniture every day. I let it settle on the furniture and I don't disturb it. It doesn't bother me. I have other things I would rather be doing. About once a week or so my conscience bothers me and I dust furiously.

As I look back over the years, I see that dust has played a large part in my life. If it was allowed to accumulate, I wasn't a good housekeeper. Back when I was young, being a good housekeeper was important. I was a minister's wife, and people came to the parsonage on unannounced visits. A lot of them looked to see if there was dust on the furniture.

Life has been much more than that, of course. Dusting has been only a minor annoyance. I have done more important things. I have raised children, and I have battled my own doubts and onslaughts of unbelief. I have taught Bible study classes and cried, "O Lord, teach me!"

Like any woman who has reached sixty-five and beyond, I can look back on a good life, but one that has had its share of tragedy and unhappiness and soul-wrestling problems. I have gone to God in prayer many, many times; and He has held me up through it all. Because of Him I have survived. I have slipped and nearly fallen; I have doubted; I have cried.

And now all I have to look forward to is to return to dust? That's my reward? Instead of God telling me there will be no more dust in my life (Doesn't that sound like heaven?), He is telling me that I shall become dust.

Dust has no value whatsoever. I never heard of anyone recycling dust. There are spray cans of stuff that promise to rid your house of dust. I could cry just thinking about the fact that dust is what I will become.

I was raised a Christian and I married a Christian, and I have tried to live the way I'm supposed to live. I have loved others and I give a tithe to my church and I have gone often in prayer for comfort and direction. Very few Sunday mornings of my life have not been spent in church. It hasn't always been easy, either.

There have been people in my life whom I have not been able to love as myself; there have been times when going God's way hasn't looked nearly as attractive as going my way. Sometimes I traveled wrong paths. I thank God for always leading me back to the way I should have gone.

Now I am growing old, and I know that I have more time behind me than before me. It's a sobering thought. Even more sobering is the fact that my so-called reward is to become a pile of dust!

Growing old is not a whole lot of fun. It takes strength and faith and courage and patience to handle the onslaughts of old age. And to face our certain death. The young may die—the old must. Either we believe it's all right or we despair.

I am so glad that dust isn't the final verdict. Of course, the physical part of me that is wearing out and sagging down and hurting will return to dust. So what? When I look at what has happened to my body over the years, I can't see any reason for preserving it into eternity.

I look at a snapshot of a very young woman. She is sitting on a white swing in the sunshine and smiling into the camera. Her hair is dark and thick and shiny. Her eyes sparkle and her smile is open and sweet. A lovely young girl. Now, someone who looks like that might be worth preserving.

But that lovely young girl was me many years ago, and I don't look like that anymore. What I am now isn't particularly lovely. People try to tell us that there is beauty in a wrinkled old face and that God has kissed our hair with white, but it is extremely difficult for me to look at it that way.

I used to wonder why God makes us go through the aging process. Why can't we stay beautiful and die in our time, but die beautiful?

I suppose it could be so that we can come to the realization that our physical selves are not important. Our bodies only house the important part of us. Our bodies are the shells, and the older we get, the more aware of this we become. We may have been vain in our youth and spent many hours and many dollars on our beauty, but age has straightened that out!

I talk a lot about some of the dear people in my

life who are now dead. It's the happy, loving, funny things that come to mind. "I will never forget the day your father slipped on that rug!" or "My father used to read Emerson's essays to me" or "She was such a generous person" . . . "He was so full of love" . . . "She was always so happy." Those are the memories that bubble up and keep us talking about loved ones who are gone. These are the memories your loved ones will have and talk about after you die. Now is the time to make sure they have a wealth of wonderful memories of you.

What does it matter that our bodies return to dust? The part of us that loves God will live forever. We can be at peace with that knowledge.

CHAPTER 30:

One Person's Choice

When my mother died, it was entirely unexpected. She was just sixty-nine years old and, we thought, in good health.

One minute we were sitting at the dinner table talking and laughing, and the next minute she was garbling some nonsense I couldn't understand.

Within the next few hours, at the hospital, I held her in my arms as a series of strokes took all of her faculties. Then she was dead.

It is not easy to watch your mother die, but I can tell you something that is almost as difficult: trying to wade your way through the talk of funeral home directors.

Especially if you are a widow with four young children and your mother had no money, nothing of material value. Had, in fact, been living with you and been supported by you.

The absolute horror of being forced to look at beautiful pastel chiffon dresses that cost more than any dress my mother owned in her lifetime. Looking at very expensive satin-lined boxes for her "eternal rest." Being asked which pair of new shoes you want to buy.

The decisions go relentlessly on, and the tab amounts to thousands of dollars.

In my grief I still had to think and act in as sensible a way as possible. I had to tell myself that I had been good to my mother in every way I could while she lived. The trip out had to be as inexpensive as possible.

So my mother was buried in one of her own dresses; her casket was the least expensive; the plot of land into which her casket was lowered was the cheapest available.

Still, I had to endure the days of decision making, and I had to pay hundreds of dollars I didn't have. For a long time after her death I was still paying for her funeral.

I resolved then that my children were not going to go through this grueling experience when I die.

And they won't. I gave this a lot of thought. I prayed about it and I talked to my pastor about it. You may not agree with my solution. I am not saying that mine is the only one or the best one. It is the one for me.

I called a person who represented a Guardian Plan. (They don't call a spade a spade either! Why can't they call it a predeath plan? Or a disposal plan?)

The representative came to my home and showed me my options. All I had to do was choose a plan, then pay a certain amount each month until the amount was paid in full. If I died before I had paid it all, my heirs could pay the balance and have the plan I had chosen.

Fine! Sounded good to me. However, I felt less and less happy about it as the representative turned the pages of the big book of photographs and details and costs.

Beautiful, lavish dresses, gleaming, expensive caskets, costs of embalming, makeup for the face, a plot in the ground. On and on it went, and the costs added up to an exorbitant amount.

I closed the book. "This is ridiculous!" I said. "It seems like a pagan ritual. I haven't had that much expensive attention paid to me in my whole life!"

Reluctantly, the representative turned to the last section of the book. "We do have this plan. It costs well under one thousand dollars. No clothes. No casket, no embalming, no burial plot. Cremation."

I had never considered this option. I did now. I told the representative I would get back to her.

I talked to each of my children. I told them to discuss it and think about it and then let me know if it would be all right with them. I didn't want to make any arrangements that would upset them or make them unhappy.

I talked with my pastor. I discovered that the church takes no stance whatever for or against cremation.

I prayed about it and rose from my knees knowing that it was all right.

There is nothing in Scripture denouncing cremation. It is our soul that goes to heaven, and we have been promised new bodies. The shell we leave behind is unimportant. It houses our self for the years of our lifetime, but at death its job is finished. Also, in an already crowded world, we do not need to use space for cemeteries. In fact, I don't like most cemeteries. I have heard of segregated cemeteries, and cemeteries with no-smoking sections. Some have elaborate stone statues that cost enough money to feed a small town of hungry children.

I have never visited my husband's or my mother's graves. That's not where they are. I can't think of them as being there, in a hole in the ground.

My children didn't take long at all to tell me that they are satisfied with my plan. They understand and they agree. I told them that they can have a memorial service in the church before they go to the beach with my ashes if they want to. Or they don't have to do that. I like it very much that it's up to them. If they decide not to, for whatever reason, then they won't be forced into doing something they don't want to do. Which would make the memorial service far from meaningful. If they decide to do it, it will have to be because of their own desire.

I am sure that a lot of people, maybe most people, will not agree with me. However, it is right for me.

I pay about eleven dollars a month until I have paid a total of about seven hundred dollars. Maybe it will be paid in full a long time before I die, maybe it won't. It doesn't matter. No matter what the balance is, it will be a small amount.

My children won't have to experience the ordeal that I did in order to take care of those last details of death. They are only the disposal details, and we refuse to glorify them.

My children and I talk about it once in a while and we all feel good about it. I told them that I would like them to celebrate my death.

My son grinned and said, "You mean have a party, Mom? With cake and balloons?"

I told him that would be fine if that's what they wanted to do. I asked them to look at my life and at what I tried to be to them, and if they can't celebrate my death, I made a whopper of a mistake somewhere down the line.

I told them that maybe they will be able to be together, with their arms around each other, close in love, and go to the beach. They can remember a few happy and good things about me and then let my ashes mingle with the sand.

They think that's a good idea.

CHAPTER 31:

Is Suicide an Answer?

Suicide is a subject I would rather skip. I would prefer to look the other way and pretend that the option of suicide is so rare and so unthought of that there is no point in even mentioning it.

If only I could do that! The truth is that, with our increasing longevity, too many of us are considering this way of painlessly making an exit.

A TV show told of older couples making trips to Mexico, buying prescription drugs, and stockpiling them. They showed shoe boxes filled with drugs, drawers full. In a calm, relaxed way, these people explained that they had no intention of spending painful months in a hospital, attached to tubes and machines. They did not want to use up all their money on a few last, horrible months. If they became hopelessly ill, or crippled, or unable to care for themselves, they had their stockpile of drugs to assure them of a hasty farewell.

You could see that this knowledge gave them a certain peace of mind.

Only a few years ago I wouldn't have written (or thought much) about this subject. Suicide is wrong; it's a sin; it's against the law; only God has the right to take a life. However, the scene is changing, and we have to look more closely. I keep thinking of the confident sense of peace revealed in the faces of those elderly stockpilers.

So often, when an old person finally dies, providing he or she has lived a long time, there is a deep feeling of relief mixed with the sadness.

"My parents assured me that they were leaving everything to me. They had a mortgage-free house, and cars and money in the bank. By the time they finally died, most of the money had been spent on their care, and I was seventy years old myself."

"I have lived too long. I'm tired. I wish the Lord would take me." I listened to a man in his nineties say those words, and he meant them.

After sixty-five years of marriage, the eighty-five-year-old woman let her husband know that it was time for him to die. He got the silent message and gave up his will to live. Still, it took almost a year for him to die.

The experts are just beginning to explore this phenomenon of people living for so long. They are trying to answer the questions of what to do with the elderly, where to put them, how to get along with them and care for them. They are exploring the possibilities and options available to old people. And they are telling them of all the things they can do so that they live even longer.

Still, some elderly are planning their deaths in advance. Some are drinking/eating/smoking themselves to death.

I tried to picture myself as much older than I am, feeble, very lonely. I am living alone, and none of my children live nearby. One day drags into the next. I don't care anymore about exercising, or going out, or doing much of anything except getting through another day. I read, watch TV, I eat a few tasteless meals.

I have money in the bank to leave to my children. I think of each of them, their particular circumstances, and know that they will be able to use that money. I would like to give it to them now, when they need it, but I must hang on to it. I may become ill, or I may fall and break something; I may not be able to take care of myself. That money has to be there in case.

I try to look ahead. What if I live for another ten years? Or fifteen? For what? If I die now, my children will cry and feel sad, but in the next breath they will say, "Oh, but she lived a full, long life." I know that there will be relief mingled with their tears. I can't blame them for that. Maybe they aren't doing much for me, but they love me, and in their consciousness all the time is the fact that they have an old mother, growing older, and they are never without at least a little prick of worry.

Then I think back over my life up to the time I reached a certain age and beyond, and I can see that the quality of my life has been downhill from that time on. At the most charitable, it has not been uphill in any way.

So why do I hang around, taking up space, nourishing this old body? Wouldn't I be doing everyone, including myself, a favor to slip out of life?

I spent one whole day reflecting on this, arguing with myself, trying to come to a right and sensible conclusion. I wanted not to offer you platitudes, and dog-eared sayings, but to try to understand the mind and emotions and reasoning of an old person contemplating suicide.

I will admit that it was frightening because at the end of the day I was telling myself that yes, I could see why suicide could be an answer. That it could almost be the only answer, and that the decision to do it could bring peace.

The next day I thought about my mother-in-law, who is ninety-three years old, lives alone, and is a happy, active woman. She brings joy to our lives simply because she's here.

I thought about the famous people—actors, actresses, musicians, artists, writers—who are past seventy and still producing, still entertaining, still creating.

I thought about my motto as a writer: Never, ever, ever give up!

My daughter called me. She told me all about her troubles, her triumphs, her hopes for the future. "I just needed to hear your voice, Mom," she said.

I remembered my son telling me that I was a together lady and he couldn't see himself ever feeling sorry for me.

For many years I had worked very hard at teaching my children how to face life. My main job was to prepare them to face life after leaving my nest. I did the best I could, by training and by example, and I did a good job. My children are strong, independent, moral, and upright. They have made some whopping mistakes, and they have bounced back. I am proud of them, and if, now and then, one of them says in a moment of success, "I owe it all to you, Mom," I am proud of that, too.

So I finally saw that suicide makes no sense. I have to remain strong. I can't undo all the foundations I have laid over the years. I can't go out like a coward, telling my children that everything I taught them was a lie. I told them to be strong, keep your chin up, fight back, don't ever lose hope. Have confidence in yourself. Know that God loves you. They believed me, and these attitudes became a part of them. I can't let them down now by taking the easy way out.

My life must mean something, and if I nullify all the good in one cowardly, easy out, I will invalidate what I taught them.

E. Jane Mall

Today you may feel that the only thing for you to do is to use your stockpile of drugs and get out. Wait until tomorrow and see how you feel about hearing a bird's sweet song, or a gentle rain feeding the earth, or feeling the sun on your back.

A stockpile is a good thing to have. But rather than drugs to kill yourself, how about a stockpile of another sort? You have beautiful memories, and it's all right to dwell on them. There are things and people all around you every day to be enjoyed. What about the example you are setting for the ones you love? You should be proud to maintain that.

When I take my daily morning walk, I pass an elderly man doing the same thing. He is frail and he sort of shuffles along. I complete one mile in twenty minutes. I don't know how long it takes him to complete the same mile, but he is still shuffling along long after I have gone home. There is something beautiful about this old man, and though I don't know his name, I love him. He obviously is not a quitter, and you have to admire that.

Every year thousands upon thousands of people slowly and painfully die while attached to tubes and machines.

I can't believe anyone would opt for this method of dying. We have read about this, many have watched loved ones die in this manner, and now at last something is being done about it.

Most states have laws that give competent adults the right to refuse medical care that is designed to keep them alive.

A living will can be crucial, one of the most important things you can do. "Competent adult" means that you understand what is happening and you are able to make an intelligent choice about your care and treatment. However, many times disease renders a person incompetent and unable to make decisions. In these cases, a living will is very important.

A living will is simply a letter written to family and doctors stating that you are fully competent and in command of all your faculties and that you do not want any life-prolonging methods used if and when your physical condition is such that there is no hope for recovery. This letter expresses your wishes, not those of your family or friends or doctor.

You may only request that life-prolonging steps not be taken. You cannot request that your life be taken.

You don't have to go to a lawyer to help you write a living will. However, you do have to write it in the form prescribed by the state in which you live. Check with your senior legal aid office or Area Agency on Aging. (If your state does not have a living will statute, write one anyway. Many times the courts will still uphold the provisions of a legal living will.)

When you have written and signed your living will, have copies made and give these to members of your family, your doctor, and perhaps some of your trusted friends. Keep the original with your other important papers.

If you write to the Society for the Right to Die, 250 West 57 Street, Room 323, New York, New York 10107, they will send you, free of charge, the correct living will form for your state. Be sure and enclose a self-addressed, stamped business-size envelope.

So live your life to the fullest and be aware of the things you want to leave behind, like sweet memories and love and kindness. Even if you're not writing a book, or painting a masterpiece, or composing a piece of music, you have something important to do, and that is to set an example. Let your children and others who love you know that life is worth living and old age is not so terrible that it must be ended with a cowardly act.

Recently I talked to a young person whose father had committed suicide. I said, "I am so sorry, but I guess he had his reasons."

The young man's mouth was etched with bitter lines. "I don't care what his reasons were," he said. "It was the most selfish thing he could possibly have done."

SECTION VI

Discover New Things to Do

CHAPTER 32:

Write a Family History

One old lady's son had married a wealthy woman. One whose family was very proud of their heritage. They had traced their family tree back to the year 1400, and they were all very smug about this.

This woman's son came to her one day and said he wished they had a heritage like that, ancestors to whom he could point with pride. "Our family isn't much of anything," he said. "Just common people, who struggled to make a living."

This old lady thought about that for a long time. She felt sorry for her son. Not because he didn't have a rich heritage, but because he didn't think he did.

So she wrote their family history, most of it from memory and stories passed down through the generations. In a plain letter-writing style, she told of the character of his grandfather, how he had come to this country from Germany and suffered many hardships. She wrote about the little mom-and-pop grocery store her grandparents ran, and of the children who were born and the children who died.

She told of the strong will and pride of her parents and of her childhood years in the Great Depression. Even the black sheep of the family was described with such love and compassion, you could feel the pain.

It was a beautiful story, and it brought tears to my eyes. Here was a true story of common, ordinary people who never became famous or wealthy but who were truly the backbone of this country. They were honest, hard-working, moral people who relied on God for strength.

This is something all of us can do for our children. Take your time, make notes, look up dates, and write a family history. Paste some snapshots along with the text. Don't leave anything out. When your children read about their ancestors, it will give them a valuable sense of continuity, and someday they can add their own pages and hand it down to their children.

I know how precious these annals can become. My father-in-law served in the ministry for over fifty years and lived until he was nearly one hundred. All I have that was once his is a well-worn Bible and a little notebook in which he entered his schedule for each day: meetings in the church, calling on members, and the fees he received for conducting weddings and funerals. I cherish that notebook: it tells me a lot about him.

This could be an ongoing project, worked on for

an hour or so each day, but it could be the most important asset you will leave for your children.

My children are adopted, and all come from different backgrounds. They would not particularly care about my family history. They know about how my father began his career emptying wastebaskets in a factory in Chicago and eventually owned the factory. They have heard about the long line of pastors in their dad's family. They are proud of these facts and tell others about what their dad was and the things their Grandpa accomplished, but I decided on something different for my children.

At the very beginning, when they were told that they were adopted, my husband and I always prefaced the story of their adoption by defining the word "adopt." It means "to take as one's own," and we made sure that they knew and understood that. Each one of the children has his or her own special "adoption story" that they have heard over and over.

Now I am writing a very special letter to each of my dear children, to be given to them after my death. I relate their special adoption story and then I tell them not only how we felt about them then, but how I feel about them now. I am letting them know how much they have enriched my life, what I think of them as persons, what my dreams and hopes for them are. These will be long letters, and I hope my children will cherish them. This doesn't apply only to adopted children! I can't think of anyone who wouldn't cherish a letter like that from a parent.

CHAPTER 33

A Checklist on Your Progress

Many aspects of growing old have been covered so far in this book. It's time to stop and think about how you're doing, where you can improve, what needs to be done. Some of your answers to these questions will be a swift yes or no; others will require time for thinking.

A friend worked through this checklist, and she copied several of the items and put them on her refrigerator door so that she would be reminded of some short-term goals on a daily basis.

In a way, these are all short-term goals (meaning that they can be accomplished in a relatively short period of time) leading to long-term goals.

For example, the one about developing the habit of planning most of your days: this certainly is a short-term goal, done on an almost daily basis. Still, it leads to a long-term goal in that once you are in the habit of planning your days, you will continue to do so and plan longer, more energetic projects.

Mostly, this is exactly what it says it is: a checklist to go through and see if you're missing anything you could be doing to make your life better. You may want to copy one or two items on a piece of paper and put it on your refrigerator door. I hope so. (There are several on mine.) Then, perhaps in a few months, you will go through this chapter again, and a new set of notes will replace the ones on the refrigerator.

The following is rather a mishmash of all that has been discussed in the book, but take your time, think about your answers, and let the results help you in your progress toward being a vital, interesting, wonderful old lady.

All of your answers should be yes. If they're not, then you know the areas in which you have to go to work. Set your short-term goals for a day or a week, but not longer than a month. Your long-term goals should be for one year. If your answer to any of these is no, set a goal so that the answer can be yes.

• Am I teaching young people good things? Who? In what ways?

• Am I showing others, by my example, that growing old isn't so terrible?

• Have I tried at least one new thing in the past two weeks?

• When I felt like complaining about my health/ age/loneliness, did I keep my mouth shut?

• Did I phone or visit at least one person in the last two weeks?

• Did I let my children know, at least once in the past week, how much I love and appreciate them? (With absolutely not one snide remark about how they don't call/write/visit?)

• Have I successfully refused to even think about whether or not anyone needs me?

• Did I spend my thirty minutes a day in contemplative, creative thinking?

• Have I read at least one book this month?

• Did I let somebody besides my family know that I love them?

• Was I a good friend?

• Did I really listen to at least one person?

• Did I learn something new?

• Have I gone outside and talked to my neighbors?

• Have I had some fun?

• Have I developed the habit of planning most of my days?

• Did I refrain from bragging about my moral purity/nearness to God?

• Have I refused to worry about anything I can't do anything about?

• Did I keep my mind open so that God could come to me?

• Did I make an apple old lady/start collecting pictures of clowns/learn about sea gulls/(you fill it in)?

• Have I grown in some way? Mentally/emotion-
ally/spiritually. (Anything besides just older!)

• Have I done everything I can to fill in the gaps
in my life?

• Have I conquered my fears? (Yes, all of them!)

• Did I set some short-range and long-range goals?

• Did I reach the short-range goals?

• Am I progressing toward the long-range goals?

• Am I happier than I was one year ago?

• Am I a more valuable person than I was one
year ago? (Not only to others, but to me.)

• Have I taken a more active part in the church/
community/organizations?

Obviously, by including this checklist, I am admitting that I hope you are taking all of this old lady
business seriously. It's true. I hope that most of you
won't regard this book as a fun romp through stories
about old ladies, enjoy a chuckle or two, and then
forget it. Truly, it's a program of sorts, and we want
to see results. When you embark on an exercise reg-
imen, you expect to see certain results. I hope that
you will consider this book in much the same way and
that the results will be satisfactory.

If you had to answer no to some of the above, I
hope you will work on those areas until all the answers
are yes.

CHAPTER 34:

Potpourri

I love potpourri. I have little pots and dishes of it in every room of my apartment. When flowers die, I add their petals to the potpourri. I also add cinammon sticks, cloves, paper-thin strips of lemon, lime, and orange peel, the woodsy shavings from the pencil sharpener. This certainly isn't the biggest project in my life, but the potpourri provides a sweet odor that I enjoy every day. Following is a potpourri of my thoughts and ideas that I hope you will enjoy.

• Just under twelve percent of the population of this country is now sixty-five or older. That is a lot of people! At the same time, we are getting closer and closer to zero population growth. It seems to me that manufacturers will begin to see the light and there will be more and more ads and services directed to us and they won't be trying to sell us only denture adhesive and bladder control undergarments.

• Our age group has the highest voter turnout of

any group in this country. That means we have some political clout.

• If you miss mothering, get a cat or a dog. Don't get a kitten or a puppy! You do not need to potty train (or housebreak) another little one and you certainly don't need being kept awake at night with a little one's crying. A dog or cat, spayed and longing for a home and a companion to love, would be ideal. Even if you never had a pet, now is not too late. Recent studies have shown that when an older person pets a dog or cat (even a hamster), their blood pressure drops. Listening to a canary sing or watching goldfish will do it, too. They don't take up much time, and pets love you back, demand little more than food, love, and attention, and will keep you company during the lonely hours.

• As we grow older, we resist change. At the same time we almost passionately worship our independence. I think being independent is a good sign. There are times when my children get very annoyed with my displays of independence, but in the long run I believe they appreciate this side of me. It often relieves them of having to worry about me.

• Sometimes I feel so young. But never, ever in the morning.

• If I haven't anything to do for a couple of hours, I read a book, or my Bible, or I work a crossword puzzle. I'm fighting brain flab.

• Walking is one of the most enjoyable things I

do each day. It strengthens my legs, and I like the feeling of everything inside of me percolating and working.

• A thin old lady I know eats twelve meals a day. However, please note that she considers one cheese cracker or an apple a meal.

• I am always puzzled by the newspaper accounts of the death of an older person that say, "He died at sixty-four of natural causes." What do they mean by that? People do not die of old age. And certainly not at sixty-four. Maybe they mean as opposed to being killed. Or they may mean it's none of your business.

• I just found out that I am a "notch baby." There are nearly forty million Social Security beneficiaries who were born between 1917 and 1921 who receive fewer benefits because of a law passed in 1977 that slowed the growth of those particular benefits. So what am I going to do about that?

• A pot of gold waits at the end of the rainbow for some old ladies. They are the ones who live out the mature years with the same lifelong partner.

• It has been said, "A man's snoring is the most beautiful sound in the world. . . . Ask any widow." And I think of: "What's for dinner?" and "Have you ironed my shirt yet?" and "Happy anniversary! I love you!"

• Did you know that you can order postage stamps by mail? At your post office, ask for form U.S.G.P.O.-1985-472-075. It's a form and an envelope. You fill out the form, enclose a check, and mail it. Your stamps will be delivered by mail in about three days. You can also order stamped envelopes.

• I wonder why God decided to start us all out new and beautiful and unwrinkled, knowing we had no sense to appreciate it? By the time we have lived past fifty years, we would really appreciate smooth skin and firm bodies and thick hair. I suppose He meant for us to be aware of the fact that outward beauty fades and we are not to attach excessive importance to it. We're supposed to work on our inner beauty.

• It takes so long to learn all that we have learned, and now that we have learned it, try to get someone to listen to you. Each generation starts all over again.

• I order almost everything from catalogs. I have studied them, and I keep track of how long it takes for delivery, and the quality of the goods. Some companies are on my yes list; I won't even look at the catalogs of others.

• I don't have a car. I only go out twice a week, so I take taxis. They don't cost anywhere near as much as maintaining a car, and I have built up a friendship of sorts with some of the drivers.

• Catnaps in the afternoon are one of the lovely bonuses of old age.

• Whenever a certain type or group of people becomes popular, they come out with a doll. There is a Rambo doll, a Davy Crockett doll, an Ollie North doll, and so forth. Do you suppose we old ladies will ever become so popular they will manufacture an Old Lady doll? What would she do? Wrinkle? Sag? Press a button and she would go to sleep?

• I have been a working-at-it writer for over twenty-five years. Can you imagine how difficult it is to work on a novel for over a year, send it to publisher after publisher, and get it back with a no, thanks? It's hard, let me tell you. My slogan is: "Never, ever, ever give up!" I keep that before me all the time. I know that a little talent and a lot of persistence will pay off. I pass it on to all old ladies: Never, ever, ever give up! Once you do, the light goes out of your eyes and you tell yourself it's not worth it and then you're through, and your world will fall apart.

• I have a friend who doesn't like to hear about all the woes and troubles some old ladies seem to constantly endure. She tells them: "That ain't my baby and I'm not going to rock it."

• There is a generational war out there. People say money should not be invested in anything for older people. It should be invested in youth—our future. They also say that having children was our choice, but the poor kids didn't choose to be born. I have heard more stupid remarks than that, but I can't for the life of me remember when.

• I don't expect anything of anyone. Does that sound like a negative statement? It isn't. I do not expect anything at all from my children or friends. That way I can't be disappointed, and everything I get from them—a letter, a phone call, a visit—is a wonderful and *unexpected* surprise.

• Let me tell you, in case you haven't figured it out, our children do not owe us their love or respect. Any parents who have their children's love and respect are not simply lucky, they did it the old-fashioned way. They earned it.

• Women who have consistently exercised their bodies and nurtured their spiritual selves don't hit the panic button when age comes creeping in.

• There is no reason why old age can't be a wonderful, happy time of life. We have accomplished so much, learned so much, experienced so many things. We have loads to be happy about.

• I read in magazines that Zsa Zsa Gabor is really in her seventies and has had several face-lifts. I say, so what? Good for her. Anything we want to do that pleases us, and we can afford, is just fine. I have also heard of women having their derrieres lifted and their tummies tucked, but I wouldn't care for the pain.

• Something new is catching on with the mature generation: mall walking. Wonderful! These smart people walk briskly around and around shopping malls, and some have measured the distance and know exactly how many miles they walk. They are out of extreme weather, safe from muggers, traffic, and dogs, and mall walking has become so popular that some of the large malls open their doors one or two hours early just for them.

• I love my church, but now when I am asked to bake 250 cookies, or run a rummage sale, or help with a membership drive, I say, "I have done all that many times over. It's the young ones' turn to have all the fun." I don't even have guilt pangs.

• I recently heard of an eighty-year-old woman who lives in her house with a young man, a relative. She is blind and deaf and spends most of her time in her room. I find myself thinking about her a lot. What would it be like to have no consolation like books and TV and radio? To not be able to sew, or look at the birds in the trees, or hear their songs? Dear God, whenever I start feeling sorry for myself, I will think of this dear old lady.

• Germans say, "Das macht nicht," meaning, it doesn't matter, it's of no consequence, it means nothing. The GIs changed it to "Mox nix," and I find myself saying that quite often as I grow older. I am all alone . . . can't lose weight like I used to . . . kids give me the silent treatment . . . Oh well, mox nix! I'm too busy doing my thing to worry.

• I thank women's lib for one thing: I haven't worn a bra in years. I don't want to prove anything; I just have always hated the silly things.

• I love it! A newspaper article told of a young couple in Italy expecting their first child, who advertised for grandparents. They were quite precise in the kind of grandparents they wanted, but when asked if these grandparents must be wealthy, they said no.

"They have to be rich inside. We just want our child to have the best of everything." That gives me food for thought: I don't have much money, but am I rich inside? If I applied to this young couple, would I be chosen?

• In Dallas, a starving seventy-two-year-old man was found helpless and in pain on a dirty, insect-infested bed. Neighbors heard the man's cries for food and water, and he was taken to a hospital. Police are looking for the son who abandoned his father. As our aging population grows, are we going to see more of this kind of thing? Probably.

• One of my dreams is that some food places besides pizza parlors will begin home delivery service. If we could call and order fried chicken or a hamburger or a spaghetti dinner, wouldn't that be great? I believe many of the Ripened Generation would welcome this service.

• I make it a point to talk to old people in the supermarket, library, and so forth. I always have a supply of the post office forms for buying postage stamps by mail, and the address and dues rate for membership in AARP (American Association of Retired Persons). I hand these out if the persons are interested, and I always receive something in return, even if it's only a surprised "Why, thank you!"

• A great thing about retirement is that the minute you open your eyes in the morning, you're on the job!

• There are more ways than one to abuse the elderly: What about psychological abuse? Treating them like children or slightly addled morons. Talking down to them and refusing to listen to them. Neglecting them so that they know how unimportant some people think they are.

• Many women aren't beautiful until they are older. Their lives and thoughts are etched on their faces.

• What's happened? On TV, in magazines, the movies, old people are suddenly stars. We old ladies are shown as "Golden Girls." We're being shown as active, smart, and sexy. Whoopee!

• If your only ambition is living for another birthday, you're in trouble.

• We know that if a morning comes when we wake with no pain, we're dead.

• If we can manage to die with dignity and acceptance, with our affairs in order, our minds at peace, we give one last, lovely gift.

• Hang on to your dignity because if you have it, you have earned it.

• In spite of all the sad talk about nursing homes and neglect of the elderly, the truth is that about eighty percent of the elderly in this country are cared for within their families.

• I for one am sick and tired of the adulation shown youth and bare flesh and skintight jeans. How can a whole generation ignore seniority?

• When you feel sorry for yourself and worry and bemoan your loneliness, your heart beats faster and your blood pressure rises. So don't dwell on yourself. Get busy, do something, and let your heart take it easy and your blood pressure get back to normal.

• Don't get impatient with the way your children are raising their children. They have to contend with many things you didn't even know about: daughters who are ashamed of being a virgin past the age of fourteen; the temptation of drugs; abortion. I wonder how young mothers today hold on to their sanity.

• A young man I know insists that religion is the opiate of the masses. Yet he said to me, "My mother's prayers for me mean so much." You figure it.

• Every time I leave the house I check the windows and lights and the stove. Twice. My daughter gets impatient with me, but she doesn't realize that it's important for me to reinforce my sense of security. I want to be sure it will all be exactly as I leave it.

• Get as close to your grandchildren as you can. Lavish your special love on them. Or don't moan and groan if later on they ignore you.

• Look at each stage of life, including old age, as the prime of life.

• Count your blessings! Not everyone receives the gift of old age.

• With the graying of America, the youth cult is rapidly fading. About time.

• The sort of person you really are begins to show

in your face at about age forty. It's either up- or down-hill from then on.

- Men my age are old men!

- Smooth, lovely, young faces are like the preface to a story. Only a hint there of the good stuff to come.

- I have no desire to keep young, only to age well and with dignity.

- I feel sorry for the young women who, at the funerals of their mothers, cry because they didn't talk to their mothers or let them know how much they loved them.

- We hate being patronized! Please don't treat us like children because we're old. We have just reached the stage where we feel we have a right to a little respect.

- Pet peeve: ads and commercials that ignore not only the purchasing power of older people, but also our product loyalty.

- Don't kid yourselves; loneliness is our biggest problem most of the time. I believe that loneliness can be a form of self-indulgence, but it's not a popular belief among the lonely.

- When I'm crossing the street and some young person honks his horn at me, I would like to remind him that if he's lucky, he will be like this one day, too.

- Are you busy laying a guilt trip on your children? If you are, I'll bet that they find it hard to let you know how much you really mean to them. Stop it!

• It's true that the checking account balances of older folks are consistently about fifty percent higher than any other age group. That's why we can often find a bank that charges us no service charge.

• A message to authors of children's books: How about making your main characters grandparents who have something worthwhile to say to children?

• My old body is okay. It's my ego that is in danger of shattering.

• Ask yourself this question: "Self, are you happy?" If the answer is no, go to the next question: "What would it take to make me happy?" By the time you have given several answers to the second question, and dismissed them (You know that money will not make you happy; you don't really want the kids little again, etc.), you may discover that you're fairly happy after all. At least, you will be counting your blessings.

• An apartment manager, talking about older tenants: "They pay their rent on time, they don't play loud stereo, they don't destroy property, they stay put, they don't party. I would kill for tenants like this!"

• What messages can you convey in only three words?

• I love you.
• How are you?
• Please come over.
• Thanks a lot!

• I miss you.
• You're my friend.
• I really understand.
• I'll do better.

CHAPTER 35:

Why Don't You . . .

I hope that you are always looking for something new to do. Preferably something lasting, which you can leave for your children and grandchildren to enjoy. Once each of them has an afghan you have crocheted, and a set of your homemade pot holders, and all the embroidered towels they can use, you start looking around for something else to do. Also, it's wonderful therapy for you.

Following are a couple of suggestions. I'm sure you have many more ideas, but these could keep you busy for some time.

• Make a family telephone directory for your young grandchildren. In a loose-leaf or spiral notebook, print large phone numbers alongside snapshots of the people who belong to the numbers. Alphabetize the book to make the kids work a little bit.

• Record your family history, sweet and bittersweet memories, on tape. You will have to go through

family albums and get certain dates lined up in chron-
ological order; search your memory; perhaps call or
write to some relatives for information. Organize the
facts and dates, who did what and when, so that you
have a picture of your family through several generations. As already suggested, you can put all this into
a book, with snapshots, but putting it on tape will be
a little different. Speak clearly, as though you're telling
a story to someone, and interject your feelings about
certain events and people. When you talk about a
person or happening that brought you a lot of joy, or
when you tell of something painful and sad, allow your
emotions to show. This may take several tapes. Label
them and put them in a safe place. You can also have
your tapes duplicated (or do this yourself) so that there
is one set for everyone you want to have a set.

• Keep a diary. At the end of each day, write in
it only the happy things, the funny things that happened. When you have great thoughts of love and
gratitude for certain people, write those down. After
your death, how wonderful for a daughter to read that
you really did appreciate the loving things she did for
you. The son who reads that his letters and phone
calls were very special to you will smile in remem-
brance. Let your diary be a testimony to the fact that
old age can be a marvelous experience. If you have
had a bad day and you're feeling sorry for yourself,
don't write in your diary that day. Take a walk instead.

• Keep a scrapbook or photo album or two handy.

When you receive the news that a grandchild is expected, start a diary: write in it how you feel about this child who is not here yet, perhaps your dreams and hopes for him or her. Write about the things that are going on in the world, what's on TV, which movies are popular. If a world-shaking event occurs, paste newspaper accounts of it in the scrapbook. Write about the weather, the price of things like eggs and bread and cars.

Record things the child's parents say or write about the child they will soon have. On the day of the birth, add the front page of the newspaper to the book, plus how you received the news of his or her birth. The child's parents will have the pictures, snapshots, baby books. Your contribution (maybe given to the child on some future birthday) will be a very special Grandma gift.

Afterglow

You have just finished reading *And God Created Wrinkles*. Now I would like to hear from you. I know that old ladies have marvelous stories to tell, and I would love to hear yours.

Maybe you have ideas on some of the things I wrote about and want to tell me about them. I would love hearing of any ways in which this book helped you to have a better/happier/more peaceful life.

Perhaps you disagree with some of the ideas I have put forth. I would like to hear about that, too. I know that you have a lot of happy, funny, sad, creative thoughts and ideas, and I hope you will share them with me.

One chapter is missing from this book. I tried to cover all the aspects of aging, but there is one I found I couldn't write about, and it is the subject of cooking for one. I haven't figured out how to handle this and, to date, have thrown away more food than I have eaten. My only solution so far is to be sure I have on hand a loaf of bread and a jar of peanut butter. If you have better solutions, I beg you to share them with me!

When you write to me, if you enclose a stamped, self-addressed envelope for a reply, I will appreciate it. After all, I don't want to die poor as well as old!

E. Jane Mall
P.O. Box 81411
Corpus Christi
Texas 78412-1411

Recommended Reading

BOOKS:
- Averyt, Anne C. *Successful Aging*. New York: Ballantine Books, 1987.
- Drakeford, John W. *Growing Old-Feeling Young*. New York: Ballantine/Epiphany Books, 1986.
- Silverstone, Barbara, and Hyman, Helen Kandel. *You and Your Aging Parent*. New York: Pantheon Books, 1981.

MAGAZINES:
- *Lady's Circle* (Contains a "Golden Years" Section) Newsstand price: $1.95. One year subscription $7.97
Mailing Department, 602 Montgomery St., Alexandria, VA 22314
- *Modern Maturity* (Publication of American Association Of Retired Persons).

Annual membership dues are $5 including $2.40 for annual subscription and 60¢ for an annual subscription to AARP News Bulletin.

American Association of Retired Persons, 3200 East Carson St., Lakewood, CA 90712

• *50 Plus*, 99 Garden Street, Marion, OH 43302. Subscription: $15 per year

• *Mature Outlook* (Magazine of the Mature Outlook Organization). 3701 W. Lake St., Glenview, IL 60025-8205.

Members: $3 per year; Others: $6 per year.

ABOUT THE AUTHOR

E. Jane Mall, widow of former U.S. Army chaplain Carlton Mall, lives in Corpus Christi, Texas. A former consultant and seminar leader for Cokesbury, Jane Mall is a member of The Authors Guild, The Authors League of America and The National Writers Club. *And God Created Wrinkles* is her twelfth book. Besides writing and walking every day, she enjoys collecting clowns.